RSAC

D0920379

Six Rules for Success in Japan

●

Study the hierarchy on the Japanese side
and show deference to those in authority.

●

Always keep a supply of business cards
on hand and carry them with you.

●

Speak softly, clearly, and politely.

●

Learn something about Japan and Japanese culture.

●

THE THREE P'S

Be *patient*, to show you are willing to understand.

Be *polite*, to show you are serious.

Be *personable*, to show you are personally
committed to establishing the business relationship.

●

Be sincere. Adapt your style to the Japanese way
of business, but make it your own, and *be yourself.*
Nothing counts more in Japanese eyes.

GOING TO

ON BUSINESS

Protocol, Strategies, and Language
for the Corporate Traveler

3rd Updated Edition

CHRISTALYN BRANNEN
The Brannen Group

Stone Bridge Press • *Berkeley, California*

Published by
Stone Bridge Press, P.O. Box 8208, Berkeley, CA 94707
tel 510-524-8732 • sbp@stonebridge.com • www.stonebridge.com

NOTE TO READERS: This book is the third revised and updated edition of *Going to Japan on Business: A Quick Guide to Protocol, Travel, and Language* by Christalyn Brannen/BLC Intercultural, published in 1991 and first reprinted in 1997. All information in this new edition was believed correct at the time of publication. Phone numbers and addresses change frequently. The publisher would be grateful for any corrections for future editions. Please send updates directly to editorial@stonebridge.com.

The publisher wishes to thank D&B Distributing, Rancho Cucamonga, California for information about the personal hygiene system featured on page 159.

The Brannen Group can be reached via e-mail at **brannengrp@aol.com** and on the Internet at **www.brannengroup.com**.

Line drawings by Teresa Holtgraves.

Text design by Peter Goodman.

Printed in the United States of America.

10   9   8   7   6   5   4   3   2   1

LIBRARY OF CONGRESS CATALOGING-IN-PUBLICATION DATA
Brannen, Christalyn.
        Going to Japan on business: protocol, strategies, and language for the
    corporate traveler / Christalyn Brannen.—Expanded and updated ed.
            p.   cm.
        ISBN 1-880656-73-6
        1. Japan—Guidebooks. 2. Business travel—Japan—Guidebooks.
    3. Japanese language—Business Japanese. 4. Japanese language—Conversa-
    tion and phrase books—English.   I. Title.
    DS811.B689   1997
    915.204'49—dc20   96-44866
                                                                CIP

CONTENTS

INTRODUCTION

Japan is a difficult market, and it will likely remain difficult for some time to come. What makes Japan a particularly tough business partner is its strong cultural roots coupled with its rapid economic success. For the foreign businessperson, this dichotomy translates to confusion—especially in the interpersonal arena. Today, when working with Japanese counterparts, one encounters the "westernized," savvy Japanese alongside the *naniwabushi*—traditional—Japanese negotiator. This is why, when you talk to one person who has been to Japan on business, you will hear "it's just like New York," and then, when you talk to another person, you are told "Japan is the most different business environment imaginable."

Both perspectives are true. Japan is changing and modernizing, but it is still an island nation with an insular past. Its brand of business, enormously successful by any Western standard, is Asian, yet it is different from business as practiced in other Asian Pacific nations. The range of cross-cultural skills needed in Japan today is thus greater than ever before. This in turn means that the Western business person seeking to succeed in Japan must understand the Japanese cultural framework—*when it applies and when it does not*.

Providing this understanding is the purpose of this book. *Going to Japan on Business* is for the first-time or seasoned business traveler to Japan. It has been designed to give you, at your fingertips, the cross-cultural skills you need to interact with your Japanese colleagues. Its insights into protocol and language will make you feel more comfortable in Japanese business and social environments, and will help you strengthen your relationships with your Japanese clients and associates. While not intended as a complete traveler's guide, the book includes a great deal of practical information on services and transportation that will make your trip more productive and trouble-free. Cross-cultural knowledge will not only make you

Speaking Japanese

Not everyone agrees, but this book recommends that you try to learn correct Japanese pronunciation and to pepper your speech with *appropriate* Japanese greetings and phrases. This is a small but important courtesy that, if nothing else, demonstrates your seriousness of purpose. The chapter "Survival Japanese" on pages 161–69 is the main repository for language information.

In this book, except for names of major cities like Tokyo, Osaka, Kobe, and Kyoto, all Japanese words are romanized with the "long signs" (called macrons) on the vowels to indicate their proper pronunciation. ***To help you speak these and other Japanese words correctly, note the pronunciation guide on pages 162–63.***

You will find lists of useful Japanese phrases throughout the book as appropriate, such as the section "Language for Introductions" in the "Making Introductions" chapter. Study these phrases. Even if you do not speak them yourself, you will certainly hear them used often by your Japanese counterparts.

more comfortable, it will also help to establish credibility more quickly.

The material here is based on personal experience and on comments the Brannen Group has received from its consulting work for Japanese and American businesspersons. Information is given largely in summary form because the readers of this book are assumed to be in need of substance *now*. In the first section is a suggested reading list of books that offer thorough discussions of the nature of Japanese business and the "Japanese mind." But first, a few general pointers:

Cold calling. Forget it. Don't think you can breeze into Tokyo, pick up the phone, and start making appointments. Making connections with the Japanese takes time and a thorough knowledge of markets and manufacturers. Do your homework. Often, your Japanese counterpart will test you to see how knowledgeable you are. This is a credibility test.

Foreign women. Can foreign women be successful in Japan? Yes. Women engineers, managers, directors, vice-presidents, and presidents of U.S. and other Western companies have enjoyed success in Japan for many years. It is generally true that Japanese women still do not hold executive titles in large Japanese companies. However, Japan has been dealing with executive-level foreign women for many years now, and sexism is not a barrier. A foreign woman should bone up on basic business protocol and ways of positioning herself to establish her authority. My book *Doing Business with Japanese Men: A Woman's Handbook* (Stone Bridge Press) is a useful reference, particularly for pre-meeting preparation.

Attitude and preparation. Your meetings will go best if you are well prepared and alert. Don't just study your client's company. Become an expert on your own company's operations as well, and be sure to study the market. Be especially aware of what other companies your Japanese client has dealings with.

Going to Japan on business is challenging. But it's also rewarding and entertaining. Do your homework. Establish your contacts. And enjoy the great food!

Before You Go

ABOUT JAPAN

Japan's history is unlike that of any other industrialized nation in the world today. For some two hundred years—from 1639 until 1854—Japan existed in a self-imposed isolation that restricted foreign access and fostered the traditional values of its people. In the late 19th century Japan began the process of industrialization. It did not take it long to catch up with the West. While the outward forms of Japanese business and industry resemble those found in the West, there are important differences in the way work and people are managed in Japan. Like most other countries in the Pacific Hemisphere, Japan has a Confucian background that has heavily influenced its social protocol: a vertical hierarchy is still prominent, and personal contacts are essential.

HOW DO JAPANESE SEE THINGS?

The Japanese are very conscious of their history, and their enterprises reflect their sense of themselves as a people with a unique identity. Be wary of generalizations. But be aware of the prejudices some Japanese may bring to their first business meeting with you.

What the Japanese may think about themselves:

- though we still depend on import-export trade for economic survival, we are focusing our efforts toward becoming a domestic-led economy
- we do not engage in heroics, risk-taking, or defiance
- we are motivated by "what will happen if we don't?" risk-avoidance thinking rather than "what do we get out of it?" risk-taking thinking
- our identification with our group is both a comfort and a burden: we need our group for social comfort but resent it for obstructing personal expression
- our civilization is unique; very few foreigners can master our language or truly understand our ways
- we are flexible and sincere and value human relationships
- we place great value on doing things in proper form

What the Japanese may think about you:

- you are creative and inventive
- you make friends quickly, but your friendships are often shallow
- you are energetic but impatient
- you take little time to understand different ways of thinking, communicating, and doing business

- you have the potential to be a "loose cannon" or a "hot head"

HOW WILL YOU BE TREATED?

Japanese treat visiting foreigners with deference. As a guest, you will find your Japanese business associates to be courteous and generally responsive to your needs. Courtesy is governed according to social protocol. Basically, the degree of politeness extended to you will depend largely on your rank within your company and team, and in relation to that of your Japanese associates. It will also depend on whether you are a buyer (the customer is king), or seller. Japanese will usually make hotel arrangements for you, arrange to have someone from the company meet you at the airport or arrange transportation from the airport to the hotel, and pick you up at the hotel for business meetings at the office or evening entertainment. As a foreigner, you are not expected to follow Japanese protocol; however, showing you understand will make points for you with your Japanese associates and make you feel a lot more confident. Graciously acknowledge courtesies received and remember that your Japanese associates will expect similar courtesies from you when they visit your home office.

A good guest knows his place. You are an outsider in Japan. As such, you are not expected to understand fully or to impose your ways. ▲ *Don't mistake courtesy for friendship. The kindness extended to you is part of proper business protocol; friendship may or may not develop. And don't be surprised if you have a get-drunk, laugh-a-lot, arm-in-arm stroll through the Ginza one evening and the next day everyone acts as if it didn't happen. Your buddies of the evening before have merely assumed their working faces.*

What If . . .

1. What if the senior person on the Japanese team falls asleep during your presentation?

2. What if the response from a Japanese customer is "We need time now to consider this among ourselves?"

3. What if you are presenting a new technology and everyone on the Japanese side nods and smiles, while the senior Japanese team member says, "That is a very interesting proposal"?

4. What if, having discussed an issue with your Japanese counterpart, you arrive in Osaka to find no action has been taken?

5. What if this is the fifth time the Japanese side has asked you and your team members the same question?

6. What if it is your first day and first meeting in Tokyo, and you can't remember the names of everyone sitting across from you?

7. What if you are taken to dinner to a very expensive restaurant and you just can't eat the blowfish?

8. What if you run out of business cards?

9. What if you are a vegetarian and are not looking forward to the dinners planned in Tokyo?

10. What if you arrive at Narita and the next departure time for your limousine bus to your hotel is in one hour?

What If . . . Answers

1. Do nothing. Senior Japanese personnel fall asleep during presentations all the time. It is a good sign. They are showing that they are comfortable with how the session is going. They are present to show that the presentation is important, but they do not need to hear details.

2. He is saying that his company cannot give you a response at this time. They need to work through their decision-making process and get back to you. Pushing for an answer at this time will not be successful. Instead, probe for a general understanding of the timing of the decision. Say, "I understand you need time to discuss among yourselves. It would be helpful for us if you could give me a rough idea about when you will be able to respond. I realize a specific date is difficult. A general idea of the timing would be useful."

3. You may have heard of *tatemae*. *Tatemae* is Japanese for "public face." The Japanese side has given you a polite answer that means very little. Your strategy should be to probe in an informal setting for the *honne*, the true feeling on this issue.

4. The spoken word and the written word are two different things. Keeping the communication on a spoken level may lead to a lot of candid information, but if you want to imple-

GIFTS TO JAPANESE CLIENTS

Gift giving in Japan is an indispensable part of establishing sound personal and business relationships. Plan your gift giving well in advance. You will need two types of gifts:

ment this proposal, you need to communicate in writing.

5. This can be a "divide and conquer" technique by the Japanese team, but it can also be a probing strategy to see if you are firm in your position. If you are firm in your position, you should repeat the same answer.

6. At a break in the meetings, ask someone on the Japanese side to make you a seating chart with names and titles.

7. Accept the hospitality. Be interested in the uniqueness of the food, but just don't eat the blowfish. They will notice and order you something else and perhaps tease you a bit.

8. You should never run out of business cards. Always take extra. However, if you do run out, either have the hotel or your contact person make extra cards for you or take your last card and photocopy it.

9. Let the Japanese side know ahead of time that you are a vegetarian. Do this by e-mail or face-to-face at the beginning of the visit. The vegetables in Japan are delicious.

10. Do not take a taxi unless you are OK with a $200–$300 taxi bill. While waiting for the limousine bus, have a nice meal at the airport. It is not too expensive and will surely be cheaper than at the hotel.

• personal gifts—for those individuals who have gone out of their way to help you

• group gifts—for the entire group, section, or company you are visiting in Japan

▲ *Use the form on page 172 to keep track of your gift obligations.*

WHO GETS WHAT?

If your trip represents your company's first contact with a potential customer, it is not necessary to bring a gift.

If this is your first trip to a client with whom your company has an ongoing relationship, take one personal gift for the individual in Japan who is your contact or who is making arrangements for you, and one group gift for your client's company or section.

If you are in negotiations for a joint venture, take a gift with your company logo on it for each member of the Japanese team; if negotiations are nearing a successful conclusion, take an item like a paperweight that is inscribed with both the Japanese and your own companies' names.

If you are visiting a subsidiary, take along an inexpensive group gift for them—it is important to build relationships with your own team as well.

WHEN AND WHERE TO GIVE YOUR GIFT

Group gifts: present the gift the first day of your visit to an individual you know. Tell him you brought the gift for the company (division, section, etc.), and ask if he would see that it is delivered.

Personal gifts: find an appropriate time for the recipient when others are not around.

If you are involved in negotiations, place the gifts at each person's seat prior to your first meeting, or arrange to have someone else present the gifts after the session.

If your company is giving an expensive single gift such as an art object, present it at an appropriate time during the negotiations when all the key individuals are present, preferably some time toward the end of the session.

Suggested Gifts

Group Gifts

anything edible: fruit or a box of candy or nuts

a framed picture representing your industry or something particularly "American"

something everyone can have a bite of: one quality director always brings a box of cookies for the entire General Adminstration department

Personal Gifts

big picture books of the U.S. or your particular state

any items your state or area is famous for

American bathroom towels (must be thick cotton)

executive paraphernalia: wooden business card holders, paperweights

gifts for your Japanese counterpart's children: T-shirts, books, pens, pencils

U.S. sports paraphernalia— golf balls, T-shirts, caps

American Indian jewelry— rings, necklaces, tie clips

liquor, brand-name Scotch

beef jerky

HOW TO GIVE AND RECEIVE GIFTS

The idea behind gift giving is to reciprocate for favors done, and to establish an ongoing relationship of giving and taking. In general, you should take gifts when you go to Japan to thank the Japanese for all they will be doing for you while you are their guest. When your Japanese counterparts come to the U.S., you need not give a gift, because it is their turn to give to you.

If you travel to Japan often—every other month or so—it is not necessary to take a gift every trip. Your Japanese counterpart may even suggest stopping the gift giving. The best course of action is to take a gift once or twice a year as a token of appreciation for the importance of the relationship.

The protocol for gift giving in Japan is elaborate. You will be forgiven if you don't know all its intricacies. However, observe the following:

- Gifts should be wrapped, but with no bows. Wrap gifts in "business" colors—gray, brown, blue, green. Do not use reds or pinks or floral patterns that look too flashy or childish. ▲ *Do not wrap gifts in black and white—these are funeral colors.*

- Purchase your gifts in the U.S. Gifts bought in Japan or other Asian countries are not acceptable.

- Use *both hands* to give and receive gifts.

- Do not open a gift you have just received in front of the giver. This is considered bad form and could embarrass the giver. Simply thank the giver and put the gift aside to be opened later. If you are asked to open the gift, do so carefully, trying not to rip the paper too much. After thanking the giver, put the gift back in its box, fold the wrapping paper carefully, and take it all with you. If you want *your* gift to be opened, simply say so.

Gifts are presented twice a year in acknowledgment of those people, **GIFT-GIVING SEASONS** *including employers and teachers, who are owed the gratitude of the giver. The two gift-giving seasons, which coincide with the twice-yearly salaryman's bonus, are called O-Chūgen (beginning in mid-July) and O-Seibō (mid-December). Department stores devote space to displays of gifts, which are ordered and sent directly from the store. Popular items include soaps, towels, salad oil, sugar and other staples, alcoholic beverages, and china and other household items. Though once presented in person, nearly all presents are now delivered.*

Avoid giving gifts in the "taboo" quantities of four and nine—in Japanese the word for "four" (*shi*) means "death," and the word for "nine" (*ku*) means "to choke." Giving a set of four golf balls would be read as four "death" balls and would certainly produce an awkward silence.

CONTACTS

Contacts are imperative; without them, you cannot do business in Japan.

MAKING CONTACTS

If you are a small company with no contacts, JETRO (Japan External Trade Organization) can help by acting as a liaison. You can also hire an agent (trading company, wholesaler, etc.) or a consultant (management or trade consultant, public relations consultancy, etc.) in Japan to help you gain a foothold in the market. If you have a product to sell, you may want to conduct market research and then look for a Japanese firm that produces a similar product to either manufacture your product in Japan or form a joint venture or development partnership.

MEETING CONTACTS

Assuming that your company contacts are in place, it is important to follow a few basic steps before you leave for Japan to maintain a good relationship with your Japanese associates and ensure the success of your trip. Ideally, this introduction should come from your boss.

Sample Introduction

to: Manager Takashi Suzuki [*or* Suzuki-Kachō]
           Engineering Dept. No.10

from: Andrew Jurgenson
           Managing Director

re: Adrian Baker

I would like to introduce Adrian Baker to you. Adrian is in charge of the marketing group for the high-end products to be localized for Japan. It is a pleasure to introduce her to you.

Adrian has both technical and marketing knowledge and experience. She is especially strong in computer science. She holds a Masters degree in computer science from Columbia and an MBA from University of California at Berkeley. She has played key roles on the very successful Zepa and Gemini projects, and her attention to customer input is very valuable. She will be leading the team that will meet with your group next month.

Please do all you can to make her feel welcome. This will be her first trip to Japan.

- If your Japanese contacts have never met you, some form of introduction is necessary—an e-mail or a phone call. Include the purpose of your trip, why you were chosen to go, and the full names and titles of anyone coming with you. Enclose a brief personal history that lists your education and degrees, job experience and job-related accomplishments.

- Give your Japanese business contacts an approximate time

frame for your visit, and ask if the dates are convenient for them before firming up your travel plans.

- Send them a copy of your tentative schedule in Japan or, if they are planning to host you, request a copy of their schedule for you, then negotiate any necessary changes.

- Plan a detailed agenda together for all meetings. Allow time for your Japanese associates to discuss each agenda and make any necessary changes.

- Don't plan to fill every minute with your team's presentations. Allow time for "open discussion." This will be a key factor in guaranteeing the success of your trip. Too many times the agenda does not allow for discussion and the end result lacks input from the Japanese side.

▲ *Be aware that your fax will be received on A4 paper (210 x 297 mm, or 8¼ x 11⅜ inches), which is a bit narrower and longer than letter-sized paper (8½ x 11 inches). See "Sample Fax and E-mail Format," pages 112–13, for tips on content.*

MAKING BUSINESS CARDS

Prepare a set of business cards (called **meishi**) with the flip side printed in Japanese. Your subsidiary in Japan can take care of this for you. Or you can have it done overnight at most major hotels in Japan. But it is better, if you can, to get your business cards ready ahead of time. Below are some printers in the United States who offer this service. Be sure to include your title on the Japanese side (see "Corporate Titles," p. 92). Avoid vague titles such as "Consultant" or "Group Liaison." ▲ *Your name on the card will be written phonetically in Japanese script. Call the printer and pronounce your name to make sure it's printed correctly.*

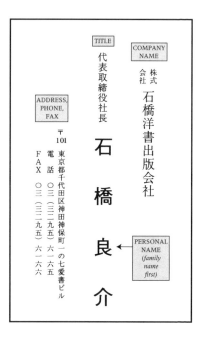

A typical Japanese business card. Often the same information in English will be printed on the reverse side.

| TITLE |
| COMPANY NAME |
| ADDRESS, PHONE, FAX |
| PERSONAL NAME *(family name first)* |

SOUTHERN CALIFORNIA
Asahi Graphic Arts
20610 Manhattan Place, #133
Torrance, CA 90501
Tel: (310) 212-7711
Fax: (310) 212-7547

NORTHERN CALIFORNIA
TechArt
400 Pacific Ave., Ground Floor
San Francisco, Ca 94133
Tel: (415) 362-1110
Fax: (415) 362-2811

PACIFIC NORTHWEST
Japan Pacific Publications
419 Occidental Ave. S., Ste. 509
Seattle, WA 98104
Tel: (206) 622-7443
Fax: (206) 621-1786

EAST COAST
Hikari Japanese Typesetting
20 W. 56th St.
New York, NY 10019
Tel: (212) 489-1376
Fax: (212) 489-1439

FINAL PREPARATIONS

MEDICINES

Bringing banned drugs into Japan carries heavy penalties. Some over-the-counter medications that contain small amounts of amphetamine-type drugs, such as Vicks inhalers and Sudafed, require a prescription in Japan. Keep medication in its original package and with the prescription and drug description clearly visible.

TRAVEL INSURANCE

Medical expenses in Japan are high, and bills must be paid in cash on the spot. To ensure you are prepared for emergencies, purchase a traveler's medical insurance policy before leaving for Japan, if coverage is not included on your regular medical plan. Contact the Traveler's Hotline of the Centers for Disease Control at **(877) FYI-TRIP or 877-394-8747** for further information. You may also want travel insurance to cover any accidental loss of belongings.

LUGGAGE

Pack light; airport and train access is difficult, often requiring you to lug suitcases across train platforms and up stairwells. You are likely to do more walking in Japan than you are used to. Train stations, for the most part, do not have escalators. One suitcase with rollers and one light carry-on bag should be sufficient.

HOW TO AVOID JET LAG

To be in the best shape from day one of your business dealings in Japan:

- The day before the trip, FEAST. Enjoy a high-protein breakfast and lunch: eggs, high-protein cereals, beans, meat, tofu. Avoid caffeine, except between 3 PM and 5 PM.

- The day of the trip: FAST. Eat light meals: salads (light on the salad dressing), fruit, light soups, dry toast. Drink caffeine-containing beverages only in the morning when traveling west, and between 6 PM and 11 PM when traveling east.

- During your flight: FAST. Eat light meals and refrain from drinking alcoholic and caffeine-containing beverages. If the flight is a long one, sleep only until your destination's breakfast time, then wake up and FEAST. Stay active until early evening. Follow this regimen in flight and after reaching your destination.

At the Border

VISA

U.S. citizens require a valid passport and onward ticket from Japan. A visa, however, is not required for Japan unless you are planning to stay for more than ninety days. If you are planning a long–term stay, you will need a sponsor, who must then apply to the Ministry of Justice for a certificate of eligibility (see pp. 134–135 for embassies and consulates in Japan). Anyone arriving with a ninety-day visa waiver will not be allowed to extend the stay or adjust status from within Japan. As the rules here are complex, contact your local Japanese consulate if you do not have a subsidiary or corresponding office in Japan to handle arrangements. Be sure to allow enough time for the government agencies to process your application; the entire procedure may take three to six months.

Predeparture Checklist

✔ current passport (allow two to four weeks for applications)

✔ visa (if staying ninety days or more)

✔ international driver's license; obtain through AAA in the U.S. (Don't plan on driving in the big cities; public transportation is faster and more convenient. If you will be in the countryside, however, or want to travel the remote byways, take a train to the area and then rent a car. This will avoid the hour or so it takes to get out of Japan's major cities.)

✔ business cards (always take more than you think you will need; running out of cards is bad business protocol)

✔ copies of health records and insurance

✔ copies of all important documents and papers (for reference in case of loss; keep them in a separate location)

✔ personal and corporate gifts for business associates

✔ medicines and prescriptions, with all ingredient and prescription labels

✔ extra eyeglasses or contacts

✔ ¥30,000 yen in cash; more in traveler's checks (remember that many Japanese businesses will not take traveler's checks, so cash them at your hotel and carry enough cash for your needs)

✔ coffee/tea maker and coffee and tea

✔ pocket handkerchiefs and tissues for public facilities

✔ *this book* (fill in the client data and gift record charts at the back; photocopy these pages as often as needed)

If you or your company is planning to set up an office in Japan, you will find a wealth of information and advice in The Japan Start-up Handbook: Procedures and Costs for Foreign Companies Establishing a Japanese Base. *Not much in the way of protocol or business culture is provided, but there is extensive discussion on hiring Japanese staff, setting up temporary and permanent offices, legally establishing a corporation, promoting your new venture, and so on. The book is available from Japan External Trade Organization (JETRO; see p. 153 for contact information).*

RELOCATING TO JAPAN?

ENTERING JAPAN

There is no duty on the following quantities and items:

- personal effects not for sale
- business equipment, samples, brochures, etc. not for sale
- tobacco: up to 250 grams (200 cigarettes or 50 cigars)
- alcoholic beverages, three 750 ml bottles
- perfume, 2 ounces
- any other goods, such as gifts and souvenirs, total value under ¥200,000

Unaccompanied baggage must be declared. Japan *strictly* forbids so-called recreational drugs. If you need prescription drugs, bring along a copy of the prescription (see "Medicines," p. 23). This can save you considerable time with the customs official.

RETURNING TO THE U.S.

There is no duty on the following quantities and items:

- goods worth up to $400
- packages shipped from Japan to the U.S., up to $50 value per package

Keep track of Japanese goods you took with you on your trip to avoid paying customs duty in the U.S. on your return.

GENERAL INFORMATION

GEOGRAPHY

Japan consists of four main islands—Hokkaido, Honshu, Shikoku, and Kyushu—whose length along the coast of eastern Asia roughly corresponds to the distance from Maine to Georgia. Japan's seashore is dotted with thousands of small islands and includes many natural harbors. Japan has few natural resources and must import all its oil. Japan makes extensive use of nuclear and hydroelectric power. The Japanese islands were created by volcanic activity and are prone to earthquakes. ▲ *Earthquake preparedness is a major concern in Japan. Always take a minute to note the evacuation procedures for your hotel or meeting room.*

POPULATION

Japan has some 126.9 million people living in an area slightly smaller than California. Even that comparison is misleading, because most of Japan is mountainous and only sparsely settled. The population is concentrated along the coasts, particularly along the eastern coast of Honshu from Tokyo to Hiroshima.

POLITICS

Japan is a constitutional monarchy with an elected bicameral Diet modeled after the parliamentarian government of Great Britain. The Cabinet, headed by a prime minister from the majority party, holds executive power. From World War II until 1994, prime ministers were selected from the Liberal Democratic Party (LDP). Voters failed to grant the LDP its usual majority in 1994, which resulted in the formation of four coalition governments within that year, the last

Five Books You Should Read

Christalyn Brannen and Tracey Wilen. *Doing Business with Japanese Men: A Women's Handbook.* Stone Bridge Press, 1993. A must for women and managers who manage women who work with the Japanese. It dispels the myth that women cannot be effective in Japan and gives valuable tips and anecdotes on cross-gender/cross-cultural business.

Robert M. March. *Honoring the Japanese Customer: Marketing and Selling to the Japanese.* John Wiley and Sons, 1990. The best book to date on how to win over your Japanese customer. It explains the whys behind the demands of the hard-to-please Japanese consumer.

Robert Neff. *Japan's Hidden Hot Springs.* Charles E. Tuttle, 1995. Instead of reading more how-to books on Japan, you should spend a weekend at a Japanese hot spring. Nothing is a substitute for eating, breathing, and sleeping Japanese-style. This book lets you in on the hard-to-find hot springs that are not overcrowded with tourists, places that you could find only if you had a friend living in Japan.

Patrick Smith. *Japan; A Reinterpretation.* Pantheon Books, 1997. Good background reading on Japan with a perspective on how Japan is recreating itself.

Robert Whiting. *You Gotta Have Wa.* Vintage Books, 1990. Did you know the Japanese have been playing baseball for over 100 years? That they greet tie ball games with jubilation? Much more than a book on Japan's national pastime, this profiles Americans recruited to play on Japanese professional teams and offers an entertaining and insightful view of intercultural relations.

headed by Socialist Tomiichi Murayama. In January 1996, Ryutaro Hashimoto of the LDP became prime minister. In a remarkable turn-around, the LDP emerged as the dominant political force again following elections in October 1996. Hashimoto served as prime minister until 1998 when he resigned after disappointing election results for the LDP. Keizo Obuchi of the LDP took over as prime minister and served until his death in 2000. The LDP partnered with Komeito (Clean Government Party) and Hoshuto (the Conservative Party) to gain a majority. Yoshiro Mori was elected LDP party president and therefore became prime minister. The party is now considerably weaker in voter support and influence over big business than in the 1980s and early 1990s when its power was unquestioned, but with the collapse of the opposition reform movement in Japan, hopes for an easing of LDP economic policies that have led to trade friction in the past have been put aside. Overall, the trend is toward a more American-style two-party democracy. Seeking to cast the LDP in a progressive light, Junichiro Koizumi replaced the popular Mori in 2001, promising to jumpstart the weak domestic economy.

Japan claims the oldest continuous Imperial Family in the world. Currently, Emperor Akihito continues the tradition as chief of state in a ceremonial capacity.

Japanese voters tend to be apathetic and fatalistic. Consumers', women's, and other activist movements are weak but gaining ground. Small grassroots organizations are beginning to have some influence on policy.

RELIGION

Shinto, Japan's indigenous faith, and Buddhism are the two main religions. Christians number less than a million. Most Japanese, however, are not religious in the Western sense of belonging to a certain sect or attending regular services, but visit Shinto shrines and

Buddhist temples on special occasions and to pray for certain favors. Communities still widely participate in shrine and temple activities.

Shinto Shrines

A *torii* gate, comprising two long poles with two curved pieces on top, generally indicates the entrance to a shrine (though shrines and temples are often on the same grounds). Shinto priests offer blessings to the newborn and officiate at wedding ceremonies. Chains of straw with cut white paper (*shimenawa*) are often strung above doorways, or around trees or rocks thought to hold spirits. Small shrines can be found everywhere, tucked into niches between tall buildings or standing atop small hills. Some households still contain a *kamidana* ("god shelf") near the ceiling.

Buddhist Temples

Japan has many Buddhist sects, including Zen, which has become popular in the West. Buddhist temples receive prayer petitions for everything from a successful birth or healing to school and company entry. Buddhist priests officiate at funerals, and graveyards are located on temple grounds. Some homes still have *butsudan*, Buddhist altars that contain memorial tablets of deceased family members.

New Religions

There are many relatively new religious sects in Japan, most based on Buddhism. Some are small personality cults, while others, such as Sōka Gakkai, are religious institutions with large, worldwide memberships.

Visiting a Temple or Shrine

Similar etiquette applies at both shrines and temples. Wash your hands at the washing place located near the entrance for ritual cleanliness. Climb the stairs to the prayer hall and toss some coins into the

Internet Resources

The best source for updated information on companies and global business is the Internet. Be aware that Internet addresses change often. Use search engines to find current links.

english.townpage.isp.ntt.co.jp/ "Townpage ": general list of Japan-related resources

keidanren.or.jap/A2J/ "Access to Japan": information on companies looking for export partners

accj.or.jp/ "American Chamber of Commerce in Japan": very useful information for companies considering setting up in Japan

jnto.go.jp/ "Japan National Tourist Organization": loads of travel information

rectangular offering box. Ring the bell hanging from the ceiling. Clap your hands twice and pray to the gods by bowing your head and pressing your palms together. Clap twice again and make a slight bow at the end. Remove your shoes before entering Buddhist buildings; step over, never on, thresholds; and do not touch religious statues or relics. Do not take photographs inside buildings without permission.

CLIMATE

Japan's climate varies from subtropical in the far south of Kyushu to subarctic in the north of Hokkaido. Your destination will likely be one of eastern Honshu's major commercial centers, such as Tokyo–Yokohama, Osaka, or Kobe. Spring and autumn are lovely. Winter averages 39°F in January and is cold enough for gloves and a heavy

Temperature Chart

14	32	40	50	60	70	80	90	100	120	140	160	180	200	212	°F
-10	0	10		20	30	40		50	60	70	80	90	100		°C

Measurements

Japan uses the metric system. Use the chart below for common conversions:

inches to centimeters	=	inches x 2.54
feet to centimeters	=	feet x 30.48
miles to kilometers	=	miles x 1.60
sq. inches to sq. centimeters	=	sq. inches x 6.45
sq. feet to sq. meters	=	sq. feet x 0.093
sq. miles to sq. kilometers	=	sq. miles x 2.56
gallons to liters	=	gallons x 3.79

To do reverse conversions, divide instead. For example, to go from centimeters to inches, divide the number of centimeters by 2.54. Another unit of measurement you will hear often in Japan is the *tsubo*. It is used for describing lot sizes and floor space:

| *tsubo* to sq. feet | = | *tsubo* x 35.6 |

coat. In June and July, the rainy season comes—you will need an umbrella. Following the rain is a hot, humid, and very uncomfortable summer with temperatures consistently above 80°F. ▲ *Even in the tropical summers, most business meetings in Japan still require a coat and tie. But you can wear a tie the first day to show respect and then, on the following days, go tieless.*

CLOTHING

Pack the most conservative clothing you have for meetings and formal occasions. You don't want to stand out. Flashy clothing (big cuff links, bright ties) on men or excessive jewelry and ostentatious color schemes (reds, pinks) on women project a lack of seriousness and respect.

Women in Japanese offices mostly fill administrative positions until they marry—and often dress very well, down to the last detail. As a visiting career women it is advisable to wear conservative suits or dresses with jackets in black, brown, gray, green, or blue. On occasion, pantsuits are acceptable. Make-up, likewise, should be conservative.

Bring clothing and equipment for leisure-time activities such as golf or jogging. Since many Japanese restaurants require you to take off your shoes, leave your lace-up shoes at home and bring slip-ons or loafers. Recently one businesswoman complained that she had to take off and put on her lace-up shoes fifteen times in one day. "Never again," she vows. Japanese public toilets rarely provide tissue, so carry your own and a handkerchief to dry your hands.

For a seven-to-ten-day business trip, take three changes of clothing and have the hotel clean and press them each day.

APPLIANCES

Electrical current in Japan is 100 volts A.C. American appliances designed for 110 volts will run fine, but a bit slower than they do at home. Most big hotels, however, have two outlets, for 100 and 220 volts, so you won't need to pack an electrical adapter; the sockets

December is a busy month, but definitely not a good business month **AT YEAR END**
because companies are busy closing the year's activities and preparing for the new year. During December, companies sponsor year-end parties (bōnenkai), *where colleagues get together to eat, drink, and be merry. Clients are invited, and this is often the time to see who is valued by whom, as people who are not in high regard do not receive invitations. Early in January there may also be a company party* (shinnenkai) *to celebrate the arrival of the new year.*

generally accept only two-pronged plugs (but since curling irons don't get hot enough, you may want to bring an adapter if you need to curl your hair; major Japanese hotels provide hair dryers in the room). Bringing coffee or tea, a filter cone, filters, and a small brew-it-yourself electric coil will save you money, since a cup of coffee or tea in a hotel coffee shop can cost as much as ten dollars.

ADDRESSES

Addresses in Japan can be confusing. Here is how a typical address is written in English:

American Chamber of Commerce
Bridgestone Toranomon Bldg., 5F
25-2, Toranomon 3-chōme
Minato-ku, Tokyo 105

This address indicates a building that is the 2nd structure in the 25th sub-section of block area 3 within the Toranomon district of Minato Ward. The postal code is 105. More confusing, this address can also be written "3-25-2 Toranomon," with the *chōme*, or block area, first.

NATIONAL HOLIDAYS

January 1	New Year's Day
January (2nd Monday)	Adult's Day
February 11	National Foundation Day
March 20 (or 21)	Vernal Equinox Day
April 29 ⎫	Greenery Day
May 3 ⎪ *Golden Week*	Constitution Memorial Day
May 4 ⎬	People's Holiday
May 5 ⎭	Children's Day
July 20	Maritime Day
September 15	Respect for the Aged Day

September 23 (or 24)	Autumnal Equinox Day
October (2nd Monday)	Health-Sports Day
November 3	Culture Day
November 23	Labor-Thanksgiving Day
December 23	Emperor's Birthday

Banks and company offices are closed on national holidays, but most stores are open. Holidays that fall on Sunday or another rest day are observed on the following day. It is difficult to do business in the period from the end of December to the second week in January, when many people take extended New Year's holidays (banks and businesses are usually closed the first week of January). Other bad times are "Golden Week," from the end of April to the beginning of May, and mid-August during the Festival of Obon, when many Japanese take a week off to visit their parents. ▲ *Avoid pleasure travel during these times as well, since trains and planes are packed to capacity.*

FESTIVALS

Japan holds a multitude of festivals (*matsuri*) and observances year-round, many with ancient origins. Most are celebrated locally during the spring, summer, and autumn months, some according to the solar calendar, others by the lunar calendar. Many include processions of youth who boisterously heft portable shrines (*mikoshi*) through the neighborhood. If you should come upon a festival in progress, celebrants may invite you to participate. Other observances, such as the ones described below, are celebrated nationwide.

Shōgatsu

Japanese New Year (January 1–3), the nation's largest holiday, is celebrated by making formal visits to thank bosses, teachers, and others who have done favors, and by families getting together to celebrate and eat special New Year's foods. Houses are tidied and debts are cleared for a clean new start. Many people make their first ritual visit to a shrine or temple, where they pray for health, happiness, and prosperity and purchase charms to help see them through the year. Temple bells ring 108 times at midnight on New Year's Eve to drive out evil and welcome in the New Year.

Setsubun

Bean-throwing Festival (February 3) marks the lunar start of spring. Roasted soybeans are tossed at shrines and homes with participants shouting, "Demons out, fortune in!" to banish misfortune and disease and invite health and prosperity in.

Hina-matsuri

Doll Festival (March 3) is Girls' Day. Dolls in ancient dress depicting the emperor, empress, and their ancient courtiers are displayed on tiers, and girls gather to celebrate and eat special dishes.

Tanabata

Star Festival (July 7) sees schools and homes decorated with bamboo fronds hung with poems and wishes, origami and paper ornaments, and shopping malls festooned with large, colorful paper or plastic streamers. These commemorate the romantic story of the Oxherd and Weaver Maiden stars who, legend has it, are only able to meet once a year across the great Milky Way.

Obon

Buddhist Festival of the Dead (mid-August) is when the souls of the deceased return to visit. Festivities culminate in *bon-odori*, dances held at neighborhood temples where paper lanterns light up the night and loudspeakers blare traditional song-and-dance music. Hawkers sell snacks and trinkets, and families, friends, and neighbors, many dressed in *yukata* (summer kimono), join together in ancient circle dances. Many take a four- or five-day summer holiday at this time to return to their family home.

Shichi-go-san

During the "7-5-3" Children's Festival (November 15) parents visit local shrines with their seven- and three-year-old girls, and five-year-old boys, dressed to the nines in kimono, dress, or suit, to pray for their health and happiness. It is a wonderful occasion for taking pictures.

TIME

Japan has only one time zone. Japan Time is fourteen hours ahead of EST and seventeen hours ahead of PST. This decreases to thirteen hours ahead and sixteen hours ahead, respectively, during daylight saving time. There is no daylight saving time in Japan. See the time conversion chart on page 173.

BUSINESS HOURS

Businesses

Open 9 AM to 5 or 6 PM weekdays. A few businesses still open for a half-day on Saturday. Lunch is generally from 12 or 12:30 PM to 1 or 1:30 PM. ▲ *When calling your Japanese counterpart from North America, remember that most of the time Japan will be one day ahead of you.*

Banks

Open 9 AM to 3 PM weekdays.

Post Offices

Open 9 AM to 5 PM weekdays. International branches are open until 7 or 8 PM.

Shops

Open 10 or 11 AM to 8 PM weekdays, weekends, and holidays. Many shops close one weekday, while others close Sundays and holidays. Department stores close at 7 PM and one weekday.

MONEY

Only yen are accepted in Japan, and it is generally safe to carry cash. You may want to exchange money at the currency exchange booth at international airports, particularly if you have bank notes other than U.S. dollars. You can also change money at large hotels and banks (open 10:30 or 11 AM to 3 PM weekdays), both of which offer similar rates. ▲ *You get a better rate for traveler's checks than cash, and you get more for your money if you convert to yen once you arrive in Japan.*

Using Money

Many stores and restaurants do not accept traveler's checks. Credit cards are generally accepted at large and touristed establishments, but most small stores will accept only cash.

Japanese pay with cash or credit cards; they don't use checks. Bills are paid at the bank or post office, or through the direct withdrawal system. Salaries are usually paid directly into bank accounts once a month, on the 25th. Restaurants, shops, and entertainment venues are usually packed on that and the next few evenings.

TIPPING

There is no tipping in Japan except for late-night taxis and rental car drivers. It is considered crass to tip a bellhop, waitress, waiter, or clerk. All hotels will automatically add a 10 to 15% service charge to the bill in lieu of tipping. Most hotels instruct their personnel to refuse any tips. A polite thank you is greatly appreciated and all that is expected.

Around Town

PEOPLE

Japanese have both a public and a private face, depending on whether they are dealing with strangers, or with family, friends, and school/business associates. Following are some observations of customs and behaviors you may encounter:

- Japanese cities are crowded. People cope by creating an envelope of personal space around themselves and will generally ignore or move away from unusual activity, such as a belligerent drunk. ▲ *They are not likely to help another Japanese in distress, as helping sets up a chain reaction of never-ending obligation.*

- People will generally be discreet about looking at you in the big cities because they have seen many foreigners. People in the countryside, especially children, are more curious and may approach you to say "hello."

- Japanese don't generally speak to strangers on the street or on public transportation, although you may be approached by someone who has lived abroad or wants to speak English with you.

- Japanese do not normally touch, though you may see young couples or young people of the same sex holding hands.

- People may avert their eyes when speaking to you, out of politeness.

TRAFFIC

Japan's streets are crowded with cars, and sidewalks are often a jumble of people and bicycles. Yet things seem to move along, however long it may take. Following are some observations about traffic patterns and pedestrian etiquette:

- All traffic moves on the left side of the road; pedestrians walk on the left side of the sidewalk. Bicyclers share the sidewalk.

- Pedestrians move along at a slow, steady pace that can be irritating if you are in a hurry. When walking to an appointment, add a few minutes to negotiate the crowds.

- Do not eat while walking (except at festivals). Standing and eating near the place you bought food is okay, as is eating on a park bench or lawn.

- Do not jaywalk. Wait for the signal to change, even if there is no traffic.

- People generally stand on escalators, though some in heavily trafficked business areas will move to the left so others can walk past them.

- Men usually enter and exit elevators before women. If an elevator is self-operated, a person of lower rank will act as operator, holding the "door open" button while passengers exit and enter.

- At banks and busy shops, people take a number for service or stand in line and take their turn.

- Lost? Stand with your map near an intersection. Someone will soon notice you and assist you in English. In quiet neighborhoods, find the nearest police box (**kōban**), which has detailed maps of the area and names of local residents and businesses.

SPACE

Space in Japan is at a premium. Here are some observations about the use of space:

- Private spaces are generally neat and clean; public places may seem somewhat littered.

- Buildings, like hotels, have huge "public" foyers with lots of unused space and relatively small "private" rooms.

- Offices may seem a chaotic jumble of people, paper, and phones. Desks, however, are generally placed to indicate employee ranking, with the section head at one end. Desks are often moved around to reflect changes in management and employee status.

- Windows are often treated much like wall space, with papers and boxes piled against them. Houses in crowded areas often have frosted glass windows. These let in the light, but prevent people outside from being able to see in.

- You may see piles of rubbish on the streets on certain mornings. Garbage is kept in the house until garbage day, when it is put out in paper and plastic bags at designated areas. Non-burnable garbage is picked up on a separate day.

SAFETY

Japan is generally very safe. You can ride the trains and subways late into the night in relative safety and comfort. If you are a woman, about the worst thing that can happen is to have a drunk accost you with a "Baby, baby, baby" or a mentally unstable person yell at you. In both cases, keep your eyes averted and move away or into the next car.

A word to the wise. Japan used to be so safe that you could lose your umbrella, briefcase, or wallet on a train and find it, right where you left it, at the end of the line. Though this can still happen, it can no longer be taken for granted. As a foreigner, you won't have to be constantly on guard, but do know that you stand out, and pickpockets tend to target foreigners. Don't be too cavalier about showing great quantities of money. Also, be particularly cautious in the Shinjuku area of Tokyo, especially in the nighttime entertainment district of Kabukichō. You may not want to venture into this area. Just looking down certain streets will tell you whether or not to proceed. If it looks sleazy, and you suspect some of the people you see are gangsters or prostitutes, this is a street you should avoid, or you could get roughed up.

ABOUT TOKYO

Tokyo is one of the largest cities in the world. The Tokyo metropolitan area, which includes Yokohama, has a population of some 32 million. The 23 wards of Tokyo itself contain a population of about 13 million within 800 square miles. In 1603, Shogun Tokugawa Ieyasu chose the site (then called Edo) as his military headquarters, attracting to the city a growing population of merchants and artisans to serve his large community of retainers and samurai warriors. For the next 250 years of Tokugawa control, Edo was the administrative center of Japan, while the older city of Kyoto remained the nominal capital and residence of the emperor. Edo officially became the capital after 1868 when forces loyal to Emperor Meiji overthrew the last Tokugawa shogun. The emperor took up residence, and the city was renamed Tokyo ("Eastern Capital").

Tokyo, like London or Paris, serves as the political, economic, and cultural center of the nation. As you travel about Tokyo during the day, you will see many businesspeople on the trains and subways, the streets, and in coffee houses. These are not idlers, but people simply going about the important business of paying personal visits on their clients to maintain good relations. Face-to-face meetings are much more frequent in Japan than in the U.S. Often the conversation consists of little more than chitchat about family or sports; it is the time spent with a client that counts.

Tokyo streets are twisted and cramped. The street layout, befitting a feudal society, was configured to keep enemies from reaching the central castle stronghold. It hasn't changed. Even today, many streets are unnamed, and addresses are not sequential. If you are going somewhere on your own, carry a detailed map to your destination, with directions in Japanese (see "General Information, Addresses," p. 34).

TOKYO DISTRICTS

Tokyo, which is divided into 23 *ku* ("wards"), is best thought of as a cluster of neighborhoods, each with its own personality. The north-

There is a kōban *or police substation in every neighborhood, at which a record of the address of each resident is* **POLICE BOXES**
kept, along with maps of the area. Police patrol their neighborhoods by bicycle and are seen as helpful rather than feared as gruff authoritarian figures. Though few policemen speak English, they can help you locate an address or lost object, or point you in the direction of the nearest train station.

eastern section of the city, around Ueno and points north, is a bit more rundown and tougher (although safe—street crime is still rare in Japan). Young, hip Tokyo is toward the southeast, around Shibuya, Harajuku, and Aoyama. The center of the city houses embassies and various affluent neighborhoods. Here are several of the more important districts:

Akasaka, where many embassies are located, is the nightlife world for Tokyo's business elite and daytime world for the many foreign companies that have chosen to headquarter here.

Akihabara, the electronics district, sells the newest models of electronic goods (some, like futon warmers, not available at home) for what it advertises as bargain prices. If there is something you want, price the item at home, then compare it with the Akihabara price. You may do better in the U.S.

Aoyama, an upscale district, has fancy restaurants and designer boutiques full of the latest cosmopolitan fashions.

Asakusa, or old Tokyo, is an entertainment district with an impressive temple gate and giant paper lantern framing a street of traditional-style shops leading to Sensōji, Tokyo's oldest temple.

Ginza, the high-fashion and swanky club district, has lots of expensive department stores and executive nightspots.

Harajuku offers glimpses of both old and new Tokyo, with Meiji Shrine's cedar-lined pathways and the trendy street Omotesandō, where avenues and alleyways are packed with fashionable shops, bargain boutiques, and coffee shops. Street-dancing rock 'n' rollers converge here on Sundays.

Kasumigaseki is home of the Diet building and most national government offices.

Marunouchi, at the center of Tokyo beyond the imperial moat, contains most major trade and financial institutions.

Roppongi, the single's hangout, is packed with expensive and trendy nightclubs, discos, restaurants, and other popular entertainment venues.

Shinbashi, Tokyo's "salaryman center" and the surrounding areas of Yūrakuchō, Hibiya, and Toranomon are flush with company offices and small evening drinking places and eateries.

Shinjuku, the eclectic area of town, has something for everyone: department stores, movie theaters, hotels, discount camera shops, a large, somewhat disreputable entertainment area (Kabukichō), and the biggest collection of skyscrapers in the city, including the twin-towered City Hall.

Ueno, an older district and cultural center, contains a number of museums, including the National Museum and National Museum of Western Art. It has a zoo, a shrine and temple, and one of Tokyo's largest parks.

ABOUT OSAKA

The city of Osaka has a population of 2.6 million. It was developed by Toyotomi Hideyoshi, a 16th-century warlord, as a city for merchants. To this day a common Osaka greeting is *Mōkari makka* — "Are you making money?" Osaka is noted for its famous feudal castle, delicious cuisine, Bunraku (puppet theater), textiles, iron and steel production, and pharmaceutical and biotechnology industries. A seaport, the city handles 40% of Japan's total exports.

Osaka, with its devotion to business, has fewer diversions than

Tokyo. Foreigners are less common. Still, the city's facilities for visiting businesspeople are excellent, with many deluxe hotels and restaurants. Communications are world class, and business support services are provided at most major hotels.

NORTH AND SOUTH

Unlike Tokyo, Osaka's downtown is laid out on a grid pattern and is divided into two areas—Kita (North) and Minami (South). Midōsuji-dōri, a boulevard running north to south, connects the two areas. Office buildings, department stores, and the better restaurants and nightspots are located in the Kita area. The largest concentration of banks and trading companies is in the Honmachi district, between Kita and Minami. Minami, in the area near Nanba Station, has the city's more popular entertainment spots. The Dōtonbori district, which runs along the river of the same name, is well known for its less-expensive restaurants and nightspots.

IF YOU HAVE TIME

Try to take in some of the entertainments and cultural highlights while you are in Japan. They will give you a better understanding of the people and provide you with good topics for informal conversation before meetings. ▲ *If you need to escape from the crowds and "foreignness" of Japan, there are plenty of American movies being shown in English. Theaters are usually close to the major train stations.*

For a current calendar of symphonies, ballet, visiting entertainers, and movies, pick up a copy of the *Weekender* or *CitySource*, free at your hotel or at the Tourist Information Center (TIC). Regular magazines with listings include *Tokyo Journal* and *Tokyo Time Out* in Tokyo, and *Kansai Time Out* in Osaka. The monthly *Tour Companion*, avail-

Sentō, or public baths, can be found in many city neighborhoods. A few have natural onsen ("hot springs"). Shoes are left in numbered lockers by the doors—one for men and one for women. Inside, an employee takes your fee. Clothes are left in lockers or baskets in the changing room. Bathers wash at individual faucets before relaxing in the sometimes scalding-hot waters. You may also see bright neon lights, often near train stations, advertising a sauna facility. Most such places cater almost exclusively to men, but despite their seamy reputation, they offer sauna baths and legitimate massages.

PUBLIC BATHS

able free at your hotel or the TIC, lists Japanese events and festivals, along with shopping and restaurants.

THINGS TO DO IN TOKYO

Tokyo Stock Exchange. The center of Japan's economic power. Address: 2-1 Nihonbashi Kabutochō, Chūō-ku. Tel: **(03) 3665-1881.** Open 9 AM to 4 PM weekdays.

Kabuki Theater (Kabukiza). The main venue for Kabuki, which dates back to the 17th century and is known for its colorful costumes and highly stylized acting. English-language programs and earphones are available. Address: 12-15, Ginza 4-chōme, Chūō-ku. Tel: **(03) 3541-3131.** Matinee performances at 11 AM; evenings begin at 4:30 PM. Admission ¥2,500 to ¥14,000.

Tokyo National Museum. Renowned for its collection of Japanese art and archaeology—especially the samurai sword collection. Address: 13-9 Ueno-kōen, Taitō-ku (in Ueno Park). Tel: **(03) 3822-1111.** Open 9:30 AM to 5 PM. Closed Mondays. Admission ¥420.

Meiji Jingū. Wonderful shrine buildings at the end of a walk down a wide, cedar-lined gravel path. The Inner Garden (Nai-en) offers quiet walks and a spectacular display of irises in late spring. Location: adjacent to Harajuku Station on the JR Yamanote Line. Nai-en open 9 AM to 4:30 PM (9 AM to 4 PM in winter), closed 3rd Fridays.

Rikugien. A fine, traditional Japanese garden, once the property of a feudal lord. This serene landscape replicates a number of famous scenes from ancient Japanese and Chinese gardens. Location: About 400 meters south on Hōngō-dōri from Komagome Station on the JR Yamanote Line. Open 9 AM to 4:30 PM, closed Mondays. Admission ¥300.

Idemitsu Museum of Arts. Displays an excellent selection of traditional Japanese paintings and ceramics, and ancient pieces from China, Southeast Asia, and Persia. Relax in plush seats, sip tea, and view the Imperial Palace grounds from its windows. Address: Teigeki Bldg., 9F, 1-1, Marunouchi 3-chōme, Chiyoda-ku. Tel: **(03) 3213-9402.** Open 10 AM to 5 PM, closed Mondays. Admission ¥500.

Nihon Mingeikan. Japanese folk art, including pottery and household items, tastefully displayed in an elegant, traditional farmhouse-style building. Address: 3-33, Komaba 4-chōme, Meguro-ku, a short, winding walk from Komaba Tōdai-mae Station on the Inokashira Line out of Shibuya. Tel: **(03) 3467-4527.** Open 10 AM to 5 PM, closed Mondays. Admission ¥1,000.

Sengakuji. Humble temple grounds, location of the graves of the famous forty-seven samurai who, in 1702, defended the honor of their master, Asano Naganori. They paid for it with their lives. This true story of loyalty, portrayed in the play and movie *Chūshingura*, has captured the hearts of generations of Japanese. A tiny museum houses relics from the event. Location: 2 minutes west of Sengakuji Station on the Toei Asakusa Subway Line.

Tōshōgū. A good place to go if you can't make it to the greater and larger Tōshōgū shrine in Nikkō, built to honor the ruling Tokugawa family. The ornate main structure was built in 1651. The main pathway is bordered by impressive stone lanterns. Location: Ueno Park, from Ueno Station on the JR Yamanote Line.

Guided tours. When you've worn your feet out and it's time to

Getting Exercise in Japan

Where to Work Out

Large international hotels offer their guests fully equipped work-out rooms, which non-guests can sometimes use for a rather high daily fee. Generally, private health clubs have monthly or yearly memberships and do not accommodate visitors.

Where to Run

The most popular place in Tokyo for a run is around the Imperial Palace grounds. The Imperial Family is protected by the National Guard. Do not try to enter guarded areas.

Where to Walk

The Tourist Information Center has a great information sheet on city walks, and you can walk just about anywhere in Japan without worrying about your personal safety. Streets in many cities are not laid out on a grid pattern, so your greatest risk lies in getting lost down the winding side streets. Parkland is scarce in most cities, but the larger temples and shrines are generally surrounded by greenery.

relax, let someone else do the work—take a sightseeing bus tour with an English-speaking guide. Japan Travel Bureau, Tel: **(03) 5620-9500**; Japan Gray Line, Tel: **(03) 3436-6881.**

THINGS TO DO IN OSAKA

Expo Memorial Park. Museums of contemporary international art and Japanese folk art and ethnology, with an amusement park, stadiums, and gardens. Address: Banpaku Kōen, Senri, Suita City, about a half hour out of town. Tel: **(06) 6877-3331.** Open 9 AM to 5 PM daily. Admission ¥250.

National Bunraku Theater. Puppet plays (*bunraku*), with teams of highly skilled manipulators coaxing emotion and drama from each doll. Popular folk entertainment. Address: 12-10, Nipponbashi 1-chōme, Chūō-ku. Tel: **(06) 6212-1531.** Performances for three-week periods in January, March, April, June, July, August, and November. Admission ¥4,000 to ¥6,000.

Osaka Castle. Built in the late 1500s by the warlord Hideyoshi and restored in 1931. Historical attraction and tourist mecca. Address: Osaka-Jō, Nipponbashi, Chūō-ku, in a park near the city center. Tel: **(06) 6941-3044.** Open 9 AM to 4:30 PM daily. Admission ¥600.

Fujita Museum of Art. Offers a rotating collection of renowned Japanese and Chinese art displayed in a traditional *kura* ("warehouse") on the former estate of Baron Fujita. Address: 10-32 Amijima-chō, Miyakojima-ku, a short walk from Katamachi Station on the JR Line. Tel: **(06) 6351-0582.** Open 10 AM to 4:30 PM, closed Mondays, from March to May, and from September to November. Admission ¥700.

Sumiyoshi Taisha. Shrine buildings trimmed in vermilion and more than 700 stone lanterns donated by sailors and shipowners, nestled like a gem in natural surroundings. Location: east of Sumiyoshi Taisha Station on the Nankai Electric Railway. **(06) 6672-0753.** Open 6 AM to 6 PM. Admission Free.

Shitennōji. Popularly called Tennōji. Originally founded in 593, the temple structure was rebuilt after World War II, but the stone *torii* gate, dating from 1294, is the oldest in Japan. Nearby Tennōji Park is the cultural center of Osaka, with the Municipal Art Museum, zoo, and other attractions. Location: 5-minute walk south of Shitennōji Subway Station. Tel: **(06) 6771-0066.** Admission ¥200.

Guided tours. Let someone who knows bus you around for a good overall view of Osaka and its attractions. Japan Travel Phone, Tel: **(0088) 22-4800** or Osaka Visitor Information, Tel: **(06) 6774-3077**.

WEEKEND EXCURSIONS

If you have a weekend free in Tokyo, take a two-hour train ride north to **Nikkō** to see one of Japan's most beautiful natural environments (lake, waterfalls, Japan's most lavish temple). Or take a tour about one hour south of Tokyo to picturesque **Kamakura**, Japan's capital city from the 12th to 14th centuries, famous for its many temples and Great Buddha statue. For pure relaxation, try **Hakone**, about 2 hours west of Tokyo, which offers stunning views of Mt. Fuji. Arrange a stay at a *ryokan* (Japanese-style inn; see pp. 142–43). Hike to bubbling hot pots, tram up mountainsides, boat across Hakone Lake, or wander through the Hakone Open-Air Museum. Then return to the inn for a soak in hot-spring waters.

If you have a weekend free in Osaka, take the Shinkansen "bullet train" for a 17-minute ride to **Kyoto** (about 1 hour by local train) to view some of its many ancient temples, shrines, and gardens. Among the more famous:

- **Kiyomizu-dera**, built in 1633 on a hillside overlooking the city, is a temple famous for its stilt-like substructure. Teapot Hill, a picturesque winding street up to the temple, is packed with souvenir shops.

- **Nijō Castle**, built in the early 1600s, was the Kyoto residence of Tokugawa Ieyasu, the first shogun of the Tokugawa dynasty, which ruled Japan from 1603 to 1868.

- **Ryōanji**, world-famous for the greatest of all rock-and-gravel Zen temple gardens, also has a beautiful pond area to walk around. Arrive early to avoid the crowds.

- **Daitokuji** is one of a complex of temples, several of which contain famous miniature gardens and tea-ceremony rooms that became prototypes for garden and tea-ceremony styles.

- **Nara**, about 40 minutes from Nanba Station in Osaka, was Japan's capital from 710 to 794, when it was officially moved to Kyoto. Many ancient buildings are situated in Nara Park, including Tōdaiji temple, which holds the world's largest bronze Buddha. Hōryūji temple, southwest of Nara, contains what is said to be the oldest wooden building in the world.

PUBLIC TRANSPORTATION

In almost all cases, it is better to use the train or subway to get around Japan's cities than to drive yourself. Japan's roads are underdeveloped, and traffic, which drives on the left, is a nightmare during long rush hours. Highways have few signs in English, road maps are inadequate (and written in Japanese), and gas is more than twice as expensive as at home.

Subways and trains are convenient for getting almost anywhere you want to go. As a rule, the subway system is easier to use than the train system. With trains you must be careful not to board an express that will whisk you nonstop to the suburbs with no warning. Before boarding, ask if the train will stop at your destination (see "Language for Getting Around," p. 60).

Do not be intimidated by the big stations, large crowds, and signs in Japanese. Major cities have train and subway platform signs in both Japanese and English. Right under the station name you'll see the names of the previous station and the one to come. Also, listen carefully to the loudspeaker on board as it will announce the upcoming station.

Tokyo, Yokohama, Osaka, Kobe, Kyoto, Sendai, Nagoya, Sapporo, and Fukuoka have subway systems. Tokyo's system runs about every 2 to 3 minutes between 5 AM and midnight—more frequently during rush hours, and less frequently in the early morning and late evening. Osaka's system is also convenient and safe, and runs about every 4 minutes between 5:30 AM and 11:45 PM. ▲ *Your host may take you to business meetings by train or subway, since public transportation is generally faster and more convenient.*

For women: When riding crowded trains, keep an envelope of space around you and avoid eye contact. When tightly wedged in, be aware of *chikan* (mashers or perverts) who may try to grab a quick feel. Though they generally prey on young Japanese women, you may be tagged, especially if you are young or blonde. Unless you feel comfortable about yelling "*Chikan!*" at the top of your voice when this occurs (the offender will exit quickly at the next stop), you may prefer the women-and-children-only cars during rush hours.

BUYING A TICKET

Train and subway tickets are sold at vending machines near the platform entrance. Maps, often with English lettering, indicate the fares to different destinations. Either purchase the cheapest fare and then pay the difference at the fare adjustment window at your destination, or have your Japanese contact or someone at the hotel write the name of your destination in Japanese, along with the names of the stations on either side of it so you can match them to the fare chart. Your current location will be marked on the chart in red. Find the station you are going to; the fare will be right below it. Then go to the vending machine and buy your ticket.

*Some train and subway employees at busy stations don white gloves during rush hours to act as official pushers (*oshiya*) to help pack the* **PUSHERS** *trains to full capacity. Be prepared to be jammed in with the other commuters. Try to stay near a door if you plan to get off at a nearby stop. Station names are announced over the loudspeaker.*

ARRIVAL

Have your contact give you detailed directions for what to do when you get off the train—especially for big stations, which have many exits. Knowing the exit number and the direction to head once you reach street level will set you on your way. If this is not possible, find out whether you should exit north, south, east, or west. Or just exit anywhere, hail a taxi, and have the driver figure it out for you.

LONG-DISTANCE TRIPS

For longer train trips between cities, seat reservations are advisable but cannot be made more than one month before departure. The high-speed Shinkansen ("bullet train") links all major cities with the exception of Sapporo. You can reserve first-class seats by asking for "green car" seating. Tickets are sold through travel agencies or at train stations.

TAXIS

Taxis are easy to find in Japan. They are clean, reliable, expensive—and indispensable. When the trains shut down, around midnight, taxis become your only means of transportation. A few things to keep in mind:

- In most cases subways or trains are faster.

- Taxi drivers do not speak English—have your hotel or other destination written down in Japanese.

- It is common for taxi drivers to stop and ask directions—especially in Tokyo, which is a nightmare to navigate by car.

- Late at night, competition heats up for the available taxis. Do what the locals do to signal their willingness to pay double or triple the fare for late night trips: hold up two fingers for double the fare and, if that doesn't work, three fingers for triple the fare.

- If you can't get a taxi, go to the nearest hotel or restaurant. Taxis are easier to get at these places, or you can have someone call you one.
- The left rear passenger door opens automatically, so step aside.
- During normal hours, there is no tipping.

BUSES

Avoid taking buses unless you are given explicit directions. They are confusing even for native speakers, and stops are written only in Japanese.

RUSH HOURS

Avoid all forms of public transportation, if at all possible, during rush hours—7:30 to 9:30 AM and 5 to 7 PM.

NEW TOKYO INTERNATIONAL AIRPORT

Your flight to Tokyo will probably land at New Tokyo International Airport at Narita, which is about 60 km east of downtown Tokyo. You will arrive at either Terminal 1 (American Airlines, British Airways, Canadian Airlines International, Korean Air, Northwest Airlines, United Airlines, Virgin Atlantic Airways, and others) or Terminal 2 (All Nippon Airways, Japan Airlines, Japan Air System, and others). The two terminals, which are about 1.5 km apart, are connected by a shuttle that departs every 10 minutes. After completing immigration procedures, you will go through customs and from there exit to the arrival lobby. While at the airport, you may wish to change money (¥30,000 is enough for now), pick up maps and brochures at the Tourist Information Center (Terminal 2), validate your Japan Rail Pass at the Japan Railway (JR) ticket counter, and arrange to have heavy baggage sent to your hotel (about ¥2,000 per piece, to arrive the next day). If you don't wish to dine or shop at the airport restaurants, lounges, bars, or shops, rent a car, or secure a local hotel for the night, proceed to the limousine bus counters to buy your ticket for the trip into Tokyo. ▲ *Don't even think of taking a taxi from the airport; it will cost you ¥20,000 or more to downtown Tokyo.*

There are two bus services: the Airport Limousine Bus, Tel: **(03) 3665-7220**, and the Airport Shuttle Bus. Tickets cost about ¥3,000. Both services run to Tokyo's major hotels, depart every 10 to 20 minutes, and take about 1 to 2 hours depending on traffic. Even if the buses don't go to your hotel directly, you can take the bus to the stop nearest your hotel and catch a taxi the rest of the way.

Japan Rail's Narita Express (N'EX), under the terminal buildings, offers direct service to Tokyo, Shinjuku, and Ikebukuro stations downtown, and to Yokohama Station. Fares run from ¥2,890 to ¥4,100, depending on your destination. All seats are reserved, and the deluxe "green cars" cost extra. The trip to Tokyo takes less than one hour. Direct trains to Shinjuku and Ikebukuro run less frequently, but you can always transfer at Tokyo Station.

The Keisei Skyliner (¥1,740) and limited express trains (¥940), also located under the terminal buildings, are cheaper than N'EX, but less convenient, stopping at Nippori Station or Keisei Ueno Station in Tokyo. From Nippori you can transfer to the JR Yamanote Line, but from Keisei Ueno Station you have to haul your luggage a block or so to the JR Ueno Station or Ueno subway station.

▲ *To avoid the Narita Airport hassle, consider China Airlines (Taiwan), which flies to Haneda Airport. This airport, which is only 18 km from downtown Tokyo, is easily accessible by monorail from Tokyo's JR Hamamatsuchō Station.*

TOKYO TO NARITA

The easiest way to get to Narita is to reserve a limousine bus from your hotel. Leave plenty of extra time for traffic. (You should reach the airport at least 2 hours before flight time to allow for check-in and exit procedures.) You can also go to the Tokyo City Air Terminal (T-CAT) at Hakozaki, a short taxi ride from Tokyo Station. At Hakozaki you can either catch a limousine bus that will take you directly to the airport or take the new JR service. Boarding at Tokyo Station for Narita takes place on the Sōbu Line platform underground. If you take the train, remember to get off at the right terminal. You may want to keep more yen to buy last-minute gifts to take home, as shops have just about anything Japanese you could desire (prices are slightly higher than in downtown Tokyo). You can change any amount of left-over yen into dollars. ▲ *Using Hakozaki as a departure point is highly recommended, since you can check your bags there for the flight and not have to worry about them until you reach your final destination.*

NEW KANSAI INTERNATIONAL AIRPORT

The New Kansai International Airport, the second-largest airport in Japan, is located in Osaka Bay, about 5 km off the coast and about 60 km from the JR Shin-Osaka Station for Shinkansen ("bullet train") connections. Designed with twin wings that extend a mile, it serves both international and domestic flights. International flights arrive on the first floor and depart from the fourth. A concourse on the second floor connects the passenger terminal building and the railway station. JR West and Nankai airport express trains arrive and depart on the first floor of the train station.

OSAKA, KOBE, AND KYOTO
TO NEW KANSAI INTERNATIONAL AIRPORT

From Osaka

There are many ways to get to the airport. Some of the more popular include JR Haruka Express trains (all reserved seating) from JR Shin-Osaka Station, which take about 50 minutes and cost ¥2,930. The Nankai Rapi:t ("ra pet") Limited Express from Nankai Nanba Station takes about 29 minutes, runs every half hour, and costs ¥1,250. Deluxe "green car" fares are ¥250 higher. Limousine buses scheduled every 30 minutes from JR Osaka Station or Kintetsu Uehonmachi Station via major hotels take about 60 minutes to the airport and cost about ¥1,300. They also link Kansai International with Osaka Airport every 30 minutes, an 80-minute trip for ¥1,700.

From Kobe

JR Shin-Kobe Station or Sannomiya Station and Kobe City Air Terminal are connected by public bus. The 20-minute trip costs ¥400. You can then transfer to the ferry, which runs every hour, costs ¥2,200, and takes 30 minutes. Tel: **(078) 306-2411**.

A limousine bus also runs from JR Shin-Kobe Station or Sannomiya Station to the airport every 30 minutes for ¥1,800, but takes 90 minutes or more to get there, depending on traffic.

You can also take the train from Kobe to Osaka, and then use an Osaka access to get to the airport.

From Kyoto

A limousine bus runs five times daily from the JR or Keihan Line at Uji Station directly to the airport. All seats are reserved. Tel: **(0120) 82-1000**, toll free. The trip costs ¥2,300 and takes 1 hour 45 minutes.

You can also take the train from Kyoto to Osaka, and then use an Osaka access to get to the airport.

REGIONAL INTERNATIONAL AIRPORTS

FUKUOKA AIRPORT

Airport access is swift on the subway line, which runs every 3 to 8 minutes from Hakata Railway Station for about ¥220 for the 5-minute trip. Taxis run to about ¥5,000, depending on traffic.

NAGOYA (KOMAKI INTERNATIONAL AIRPORT)

Shuttle buses arrive and depart the airport every 10 to 15 minutes for the Nagoya Bus Center (JR Nagoya Station). The 18-km ride, which takes about 45 minutes, costs about ¥700.

NIIGATA AIRPORT

Catch a bus for the 30-minute ride for a ¥300 fare.

OSAKA (ITAMI INTERNATIONAL AIRPORT)

Bus service to and from downtown Osaka takes 30 minutes and costs ¥510. Service to JR Shin-Osaka Station takes 25 minutes and costs ¥400.

SAPPORO INTERNATIONAL AIRPORT (CHITOSE AIRPORT)

The bus ride to and from the city takes about 70 minutes for a ¥750 fare. The Chitose Line's Airport Express takes 35 minutes for ¥940.

TOKYO (HANEDA AIRPORT)

The Tokyo monorail whisks you from JR Hamamatsuchō Station to Haneda, or back again, in 23 minutes for ¥460.

LANGUAGE FOR GETTING AROUND

ASKING FOR DIRECTIONS

Sumimasen.
Excuse me.

[PLACE] *wa doko desu ka?*
Where is the (PLACE)?

eki	train station
ginkō	bank
otearai	restroom
yūbinkyoku	post office

Koko kara aruite ikemasu ka?
Can I walk there from here?

Koko wa doko desu ka?
Where am I?

TRAINS

*Shinjuku eki **wa doko desu ka?***
Where is *Shinjuku Station*?

*Shinjuku **kara** Harajuku **made no kippu wa ikura desu ka?***
How much is a ticket from *Shinjuku* to *Harajuku*?

Common Signs in Japanese

北	north	男	man	円	yen
南	south	女	woman	上	up
東	east	出口	exit	下	down
西	west	入口	entrance	地下鉄	subway
止	stop	非常口	emergency exit	電車	train

Kono densha wa [DESTINATION] *e ikimasu ka?*
Does this train go to [DESTINATION]?

TAXIS

Ikebukuro **onegai shimasu.**
Please take me to *Ikebukuro*.

Kono jūsho onegai shimasu.
Please take me to this address.
(Show address or map in Japanese.)

Tōi desu ka?
Is it far from here?

Ikura desu ka?
How much is it?

Koko de tomete kudasai.
Please stop here.

Koko de sukoshi matte kudasai.
Please wait here for a little while.

Arigatō gozaimasu.
Thank you.

DOORMAN

Takushī onegai shimasu.
Please help me get a taxi.
(It's nice to know that the word for "taxi" in Japanese is *takushī*.)

Tetsudatte kudasai.
Please help me.

Doko ka resutoran o shōkai shite kudasaimasen ka?
Can you recommend a restaurant to me?

Depāto wa kono chikaku ni arimasu ka?
Is there a department store nearby?

Eki wa doko desu ka?
Where is the station?

AT THE HOTEL

At any major hotel in Japan, you should relax and speak English. This is not the place to try out your Japanese. Most hotel personnel have been hired especially for their English-language ability and things will flow more smoothly if you make your requests and inquiries in English.

MONEY

You will have no problem using a credit card (Diner's Club, American Express, Visa, MasterCard) at major Japanese hotels. Many restaurants and shops, however, will only accept cash. Even traveler's checks are often a problem. ▲ *Before leaving your hotel for the day, cash some traveler's checks at the hotel cashier. It is a lot less trouble, and the rates at the hotel are comparable to those at the bank. Feel reasonably safe carrying cash, but watch for pickpockets on the train.*

TIPPING

There is no tipping in Japan except for late-night taxis and rental car drivers (see "Tipping," p. 38).

AT THE RESTAURANT

If you are on your own and are wondering what to eat, look for restaurants with plastic food in their windows. Probably the best place to eat solo, besides the coffee shop at your hotel, is at a large department store. There is usually a floor with several different restaurants. You can bring the waiter or waitress out to the food display and point to what you want to eat. Be careful about the prices, as the numbers will often be written in Japanese. Generally, noodles and spaghetti are fairly reasonable, while tempura, sushi, *sashimi*, and steak can be expensive.

PAYING

Your tab is usually tallied on a bill clipped onto a plastic backing that is left face-down at your table. The waiter will write your order for each item on a perforated strip on the bill, then tear it off, leaving a carbon copy. After your meal, take the bill to the cash register to pay. Some restaurants, particularly at lunchtime, require you to pay for what you want upon entry and then give you a ticket to place on your table. The waitress will pick it up and bring you your order. Do not tip at restaurants (a 10% tax is added if your bill is over ¥10,000).

Hotel and Dining Hints

- **Laundry.** Hotel dry cleaning and laundry services are superb. Your dress shirts will come back heavily starched unless you specify otherwise.

- **Massage.** Most hotels offer a massage service. You will be asked to lie on your bed with your *yukata* (Japanese robe) on. It's a good way to relax after stressful meetings.

- **Reserving the Airport limo.** If you plan to take the limousine bus to the airport, reserve your place two days ahead of time to be guaranteed a space. Each hotel is allotted a fixed number of seats. If you can't reserve, ask your hotel to call around to other hotels to see if there are any extra seats available. Otherwise you may have to take an earlier bus to the airport.

DINING HINTS

- **Food can be lukewarm or even cold.** Most restaurants do not serve food piping hot. Everything from soup to the main meal may come to the table lukewarm. The exceptions are meals prepared at your table and hot drinks.

- **Ask for water.** It is not customary for water to be served when you sit down. If you want a glass of water, ask for it. Some restaurants, however, do serve tea.

- **Food comes at different times.** Waiters will sometimes bring food when it's ready, without waiting to serve the entire table at once. It is not considered rude to begin eating when your food is placed before you (though Japanese may wait until everyone has been served).

- **No napkins**. Though many restaurants and coffee shops may bring you an **oshibori** (a small, damp hot or cold towel) to wipe your hands on before eating, napkins are generally not provided, except in Western-style eateries.

- **Getting a server's attention**. Do not simply call out "Excuse me" or "Waitress." Instead, try to catch the server's eye. If this doesn't work, raise your hand slightly as you would to answer a question. If you still don't get a response, wave your raised hand (moderately) back and forth.

USEFUL PHRASES

At the Hotel

Konban heya ga arimasu ka?
Do you have a room for tonight?

Yoyaku shite arimasu.
I have a reservation.

Yoyaku shite arimasen.
I don't have a reservation.

Ordering

[NAME OF ITEM] **ga arimasu ka?**
Do you have [NAME OF ITEM]?

Sumimasen. [NAME OF ITEM] **onegai shimasu.**
Excuse me. Please give me [NAME OF ITEM].

When you are at a restaurant or bar, the waiter may come by and say "rasuto ōdā desu." This means that it **LAST ORDER**
is your last chance to order something before the place closes. Eating and drinking places usually stay open up to an hour after the "last order" call. To announce they are closing, many shops, eating places, and even parks and museums play "Auld Lang Syne" over the loudspeaker.

ohiya	cold water
kōhī	coffee
kōcha	black tea
ocha	green tea
okanjō	the bill

Ryōshūsho onegai shimasu.
May I please have a receipt?

SHOPPING

It would take half a day just to check out the merchandise at a large department store, so head for the information desk near the front entrance, pick up a store map, and ask for the location of the items you are looking for. Department stores generally sell foods of all kinds in the basement and have an upper floor dedicated to restaurants. The roof area is often an amusement park for children. They have large stationery and kimono and kimono accessories sections, and often a small Japanese folk crafts (*mingeihin*) area. Ginza department stores have souvenir areas with gifts at fairly reasonable prices. Nothing is rushed, so make allowance for the slow pace. Clerks are helpful and will wrap packages beautifully in store logo paper. Packages can also be sent home. Foods wrapped as gifts are stamped with the date of purchase. Change is returned in a lump sum without being counted it out to you.

There are also tax-free shops; check out the local tourist paper for locations. The most well known are at Tokyo's International Arcade, near Ginza, and Kyoto's Handicraft Center. Prices are comparable—some higher, some lower—to those at the camera and electronics discount shops that abound in the Akihabara and Shinjuku areas in Tokyo and the Nipponbashi area in Osaka.

WHAT TO BUY

Authentic Japanese goods are the best buys. Exquisitely handcrafted goods are available almost everywhere. Some things you may want to pick up for yourself or as gifts for others include:

Japanese dolls

pearls

cloisonné

damascene

lacquerware

bamboo ware

pottery and china

kimono and *obi* ("sashes"; used items can be fairly inexpensive)

furoshiki (cotton, rayon, or silk wrapping cloths)

fans

Japanese folk crafts: paper or silk wallets, wooden boxes, Japanese charms

daruma (round, red monk figures) and *kokeshi* dolls (wooden lathe-made figures with painted features)

handmade Japanese paper (*washi*)

woodblock prints

wooden combs

silk goods

WHERE TO SHOP

A good place in Tokyo to get any of the above items at a reasonable price (they ship, too) is the Oriental Bazaar on Omotesandō, a large boulevard that runs down the hill on the right side from Harajuku Station on the Yamanote Line.

In Osaka, try Mikimoto for pearls and Nakano Shima (an island in the Yodo River) for bargains.

Both cities have rummage and antique sales on certain days where you can pick up bargains in pottery, old kimono, woodblock prints, and antique household items. There are listings for these venues in tourist papers and brochures.

USEFUL PHRASES

[Item} *ga arimasu ka?*
Do you have [item]?

chizu	map
hankachi	handkerchief
kasa	umbrella
setomono	pottery
kusuri	medicine
kaze-gusuri	cold medicine
ichōyaku	stomach medicine
zutsūyaku	headache medicine (aspirin)
firumu	film
tokei	watch
eiji shinbun	English-language newspaper
pen	pen
tabako	cigarettes
omiyage	souvenir

Kore/sore o misete kudasai.
Please show me this/that one.

Ikura desu ka?
How much is it?

Kore ni shimasu.
I'll take this/these.

*Motto chiisai **no ga arimasu ka?***
Do have a *smaller* one?

Motto ōkii	larger
Motto yasui	less expensive
Motto takai	more expensive

Irimasen.

I don't need/want it.

Tsutsumanakutemo ii desu. Fukuro de ii desu.

I don't need it/them wrapped. Just a bag is fine.

Business Basics

KEY CONCEPTS

There are a few key concepts in Japanese business that you should know. Learning them will explain a great deal—the use of silence in business meetings, for example, or the seemingly schizophrenic behavior of someone who is dignified in formal business settings and then acts foolish after hours. Five key concepts apply here that are best explained in two groups:

GROUP I: *Ba, Ma, Wa*

Ba means "place." In business, this translates to the correct behavior for the setting/place.

    Example: A foreigner working in Japan goes out for a drink with a Japanese coworker. After one drink, the Japanese starts to act in a way that doesn't fit with the personality the foreigner is familiar with at work. Not understanding what this is all about, the foreigner concludes that this is a very strange individual who perhaps should be avoided in the future. At work the next day, the foreigner cools off toward this individual.

Japanese view: Formal occasions require formal behavior. And then one can unwind in informal settings, particularly after a drink or two. Work and play are separate, and there are appropriate behaviors for each. If the foreigner backs away the next day, the Japanese may feel the friendship he extended has been rejected.

Advice: Knowing that the *ba* dictates the type of behavior, follow along. As a foreigner and representative of your company, do not attempt to be as outrageous as your host. When you get to work the next day, do not recount the goings-on of the night before, except for a brief thank you for the pleasant time.

Ma means "timing" or "space." Things are given *ma* in Japan. If you push when you should pause, you and your motives become suspect. Here are two examples:

Example 1: You are negotiating with a Japanese company. In the middle of a meeting, the Japanese team starts to speak Japanese among themselves, and this goes on for a good 10 minutes. You have no idea what is going on and no one offers an explanation. What the Japanese team is doing is taking *ma*, time to consider. They are taking this time to make a "real-time" decision when negotiating with foreigners, which is not their usual business practice. To do this, they must check in with all team members and reach an "on-the-spot" consensus. To a foreigner, this seems rude. The worst thing you can do, however, is tell them that you think it is rude. Also refrain from telling the Japanese team not to speak Japanese during the meetings. Besides seriously injuring your relationship, this would slow negotiations considerably because the Japanese team would not be able to come to small decisions during the face-to-face meetings. Many Jap-

Pre-Meeting Checklist

Nothing makes a worse impression on the Japanese than the appearance of being ill prepared and disorganized. Make sure you have:

✔ A photocopied page of the business cards of the Japanese participants. If you don't know all the participants, give a blank seating chart to the interpreter or a junior member on the Japanese team and ask that the names be written out for you.

✔ Plenty of your own business cards. They should be kept in your lapel or jacket pocket or briefcase in a card holder, not in your rear seat pocket—no crumpled or soiled cards.

✔ Gifts, if you are presenting any corporate gifts.

✔ An outline of your presentation, in bullet form and with no long paragraphs. Prepare handouts of all presentation materials, including copies of overhead transparencies.

anese, however, are aware that this is irritating behavior to foreigners and try to avoid it.

Example 2: You are negotiating with a Japanese company. In the middle of the meeting the entire Japanese team looks down at the table and remains silent—for a horrifying 45 seconds. What does this mean? There are four possibilities:

• It means nothing. They are simply taking *ma* ("time") silently.

• It is a positive sign. They are impressed with what you have just said and are giving it a respectful *ma* ("space") before resuming.

• It is a negative sign. They are upset with what you just said and are trying to tell you so. They are also wondering why you don't understand this.

✔ Several copies of the entire text of your presentation. Hand these out after your presentation and announce in your introduction that you will be doing so. This will help the designated note taker on the Japanese team to relax and not waste time on frantic note taking during your presentation. Once you know the Japanese team, you can ask if they prefer to have the text before or after your presentation.

✔ Translations in Japanese of your technical materials, product specifications, and the like. Do not leave this for the Japanese customer or potential partner to do.

✔ A pointer, if you are using an overhead projector. Never use the pointer to point at an individual.

✔ Paper, pens, support documents, correspondence, etc.

✔ If you can't stand cigarette smoke, tell someone on the Japanese team before the meeting or during a break and let the Japanese side figure out what to do. Don't complain about the smoke during the meeting itself.

• They have read a cross-cultural book telling them silence makes foreigners, especially Americans, uncomfortable. They are aware of this and are trying to throw you off to force a concession.

You may think that it is impossible to tell the difference between these four possibilities. Not true. Now that you know, it will be immediately clear to you which of the above you are witnessing.

Wa means "harmony." This does not mean that everyone in Japan walks around in some kind of harmonious state. It just means that you try to get your message across without breaking the *wa*. This manifests most often in the infamous Japanese "yes." Do not take "yes" for an answer. When you hear "yes" from your Japanese associates, it can mean: they agree, they would like to agree, they have heard your request, they have heard your request and understand it, they are trying to throw you off by saying yes and then doing nothing, they are trying to buy time. The only thing you can be certain of is that they have heard your request. You should investigate further. They are most likely trying to maintain *wa* and honor your request, no matter how outrageous it is, by initially saying "yes" and then qualifying it later.

GROUP II: *UCHI* VS. *SOTO*

Uchi means "inside" or "insider." In business, your *uchi* is your company/section. *Soto* means "outside" or "outsider."

An understanding of these two terms is critical for successful business relations in Japan, which is a group-oriented culture. Japanese gain their identity from groups: country, family, school, company. In any given situation, you are either *uchi* or *soto*. As a foreigner, you will always be *soto*. Even if you share a common company, you will always feel like a *soto*. This is not necessarily bad. A *soto* does not have to follow the same strict rules as an *uchi* and is given more leeway. As an outsider, you are expected to act like one. In fact, a *soto* who tries to act too much like an *uchi* is not very effective in the Japanese business environment.

8 TENETS FOR DOING BUSINESS IN JAPAN

1. PRESENT ONE FACE

From the Japanese perspective, the Western tendency to express a multitude of opinions, no matter how true, almost always reflects badly on the company and its policies. Even worse, statements made off-line and with no specific negotiating intent, e.g., explanations intended to show the speaker's familiarity with the issues at hand or narrations of the speaker's role in the decision-making process, are usually taken by the Japanese side as potentially significant facts about company direction or indecision in the ranks and not just as one opinion. Conversely, presenting "one face"—one collective opinion—builds Japanese confidence in your company and your credibility and will save you a considerable amount of time in the negotiations. Remember, too that each person on your team represents the company, from the director to the engineer. You are all your company. What you or anyone on your team says will most likely be taken as company policy.

2. YOU ARE NOT EQUAL TO YOUR CUSTOMER; YOUR CUSTOMER IS NOT YOUR PARTNER.

In Japan, the maxim "The Customer Is Always Right" translates to:

- "Never think you can negotiate with your Japanese customer as an equal or a partner; the customer is king."
- "Never Argue with Your Customer." Just repeat your point and your data over and over again.
- "Always Ask; Never Tell." Ask questions, questions, and then more questions to show sincerity and to gather valuable information on your customer's needs.

3. UNDERSTAND THE ROLES OF BUYER AND SELLER

Buyer: The buyer will be politely interrogated. The Japanese side will ask questions to better understand your needs. Be prepared to answer, or attempt to answer, all questions.

Seller: Be prepared to be not so politely interrogated. Your response to the multitude of questions the Japanese are sure to ask you is to answer everything. No question should be treated as trivial or irrelevant, even if it may seem so. The reason for such questions could be to prepare for more serious communication, to test your commitment to the process, or simply to explore your character.

4. PRACTICE THE SOFT-SELL: MODESTY IS A VIRTUE

In negotiations: Don't boast or brag about your company or your own accomplishments. It is not okay to say things like, "Our company has the best product in the industry, bar none, and we can prove it" or "It is true that we have had some problems with our old die, but our new die is far superior and we are extremely proud of it." Such typical self-promotion will be received in Japan as bravado inappropriate to a serious business relationship, even as an indication that there must be something wrong somewhere. Note, however, that it is acceptable practice in Japan for the vendor to present concrete evidence of success in the form of facts, charts, graphics, etc. Get your message across that way.

In advertising: Turn on Japanese television and it will be immediately evident to you that, although American-style advertising is becoming more popular, most does not rely on claims about consumer benefits and product superiority. Instead, it persuades by means of what the Japanese call the "human touch." This is also called "mood advertising," and it is designed to make you feel good. An operative contrast between U.S. and Japanese advertising is that the former relies heavily on words to get the message across and the latter on visual imagery. Tamotsu Kishii, international division creative director of Dentsū Inc., Japan's largest advertising agency, explains it by saying, "It is more important to evoke a sense of sympathy that provides a link of fellow-feeling between the consumer and the advertiser. . . . In order to make commercials that appeal to the sensitivities of the Japanese people, it is more important to devise ways to increase their interest in the product and to heighten the image of the enterprise than to use a lot of words to explain the 'superiority of the product.'"

5. *AMAE*: ANTICIPATE EACH OTHER'S NEEDS FOR GOOD CUSTOMER RELATIONS

The word *amae*, from *amaeru* ("behave like a spoiled child"), is often translated into English as "to be indulged." In this instance it means that it is your responsibility to understand and anticipate your customers' needs rather than your customers' responsibility to inform you of their needs. You can accomplish this with a lot of face-to-face time. The Japanese would say, "Do not put me in the uncomfortable position of having to tell you my needs. Indulge me."

6. EXTEND *SĀBISU*: SERVICE

Sābisu, the Japanese pronunciation of "service," is how you are expected to treat your customer in Japan.

Sābisu dos

- Pay immediate attention to customer needs.
- Provide information at the customer's request and follow up to insure that the information was adequate.
- Extend hospitality by receiving your customers graciously and making them feel comfortable. Someone should be with the customer at all times.
- Know your product and company thoroughly.
- Refrain from expressing your own opinion (unless your relationship is a strong one).
- Wrap gifts carefully yourself, or present them immaculately packaged (see "Gifts to Japanese Clients," pp. 14–19).

- Be gracious at all times, no matter how trying the customer; it could be a test, and you gain a great deal if you pass.

Sābisu don'ts

- Don't do anything that could show the customer in a bad light.
- Don't behave in an off-hand or casual manner; this could be interpreted as insincerity or arrogance.
- Don't act impatient when responding to a customer's needs.

7. ESTABLISH A PERSONAL RELATIONSHIP

In Japan, business depends on personal relationships. A great deal of time, money, and ceremony goes into establishing the close personal relationships that are essential for successful business relations in Japan. It is not uncommon for the Japanese to refuse to do business on the grounds that they don't feel comfortable with their counterpart (Japanese or foreign), even if the counterpart has the very thing a client needs to be competitive. Therefore, think of your time in Japan not as an opportunity to sell, but a chance to establish personal connections with customers.

8. NEVER SAY "THIS IS NOT MY JOB" TO A JAPANESE CUSTOMER

Japanese expect a response to every request. If you don't have the information at hand, find it or delegate someone to find it, then provide it to your customer. And, if the customer is wrong, remember that "the customer is never wrong." Therefore, in your response, simply present the facts and let them speak for themselves.

PRESENTATION TIPS

Making a presentation to a Japanese audience can be daunting. If you keep in mind a few basic ideas regarding the expectations and abilities of your audience, however, your presentation is certain to be more successful. In a recent cross-cultural technology review between a U.S. and Japanese company, the English-speaking presenters used the following phrases that the English-speaking Japanese members were not able to understand: "No smoking gun," "Coat-tail strategy," "Spots that are bumpy," "Running out of gas," "Shy away," "Low-hanging fruit," "Move up the product value chain," "Walk that thin line," "That's straightforward," and "In lieu of." The following suggestions for presenters will aid in the cross-cultural exchange of information.

DELIVERY DOS AND DON'TS

- Do slow down—and don't slow down for five minutes and then go back to warp speed.

- Don't refer to Asia as the Far East or the Orient. The Far East is a very U.S.-centric term (far from whom?) and the Orient is okay for furniture and rugs but outdated for anything else.

- Don't use broken English (dropping "a," "the," etc.). Broken English does not help non-native speakers. In fact, you run the risk of insulting them by not speaking grammatically correct English.

- Don't use words that non-native speakers of English must look up in a dictionary, e.g.: exponentially, prolific, discerning, expediently, granularity, aggregate, approximating, elaborate, etc.

- Don't use phrases that a non-native speaker will not find in a dictionary, e.g.: "killer app," "the catchall," "bottlenecks," "gory details," "you folks," "It came down to two things."

- Don't use U.S.-centric analogies, cartoons, etc. For example, the

U.S. 911 equivalent for emergencies in Japan is 110 and 119.

- Don't speak in run-on sentences.

- Don't expect eye contact from all audience members. As the presenter, do use eye contact with your audience, but do not maintain eye contact for three seconds as some speech classes teach. This might be considered aggressive behavior, making your presentation less effective.

- Avoid putting your hands into your pockets when talking.

- Do not point at someone or something. If you have to point while presenting, do so using your full hand or thumb. Never use a single finger to point at anyone. People only use a single finger if pointing to inferiors.

- Always summarize for clarification.

- Avoid:

   Idioms (unless you are prepared to explain them): "Let's kill two birds with one stone," "They are blowing smoke," ". . . come up with a design."

   Slang and acronyms: "The AT of the IT group is . . ." If an acronym is necessary, first say it in its entirely, then say the acronym and then say what it stands for again. Of course, industry-specific acronyms are fine.

   Colloquialisms: "This is bad, really bad."

   Metaphors: "We are the sun in a light-hungry universe."

   Difficult vocabulary: "The problem is exacerbated by . . .," "spin ASIC," "quandary."

   Complex sentences: "The problem, as we described earlier, really I mean only the area of concern, is . . ."

   Difficult grammar: "If we had had the means to determine the root cause, the . . ."

Contractions: "can't," "wouldn't."

Double negative statements: "It is not so common never to find . . .,""It is not atypical."

WRITTEN DOS AND DON'TS

- If your graphic will include text, do leave room for the translation (especially for the editing and expansion of text). Avoid dark color backgrounds, such as blue or gray; when copied they will turn black and leave no room for non-English speakers to translate or take notes.

- Always include a "purpose" slide. The second page of the presentation should have a clear, declarative sentence that explains the main purpose of the presentation. This will provide a topic sentence that can later be reviewed by the participants. For example, "The purpose of this presentation is to propose new technologies for Thor II and Thor III."

- If your presentation is scheduled for one hour, you should have about forty-five minutes worth of materials.

- Hand out copies of your materials before your presentation. Your audience will want to take notes on the actual presentation materials.

- Each slide should have a clear title; e.g., change "Thor 1 TMR" to "Technology considered to Reduce TMR for Thor 1."

- Include biographies for all new personnel.

- Your graphics should be acceptable worldwide. In order to ensure this, avoid road signs, references to alcohol or related matters, animals, trendy objects, parts of the body, hand gestures and religious symbols. For example, a green arrow does not necessarily equal "conclusion."

- If the data on the slides are old, write the updated information on the overhead or correct in real time on the handout.

- Measurements on all diagrams and graphics should include their metric equivalents.

- Do not put up an overhead and then verbally state the message differently. Say exactly what is on the overhead so that the people who are translating do not have to translate twice. However, after giving the same visual and verbal message, it is okay to add embellishments.

DEMEANOR

GROOMING TIPS

Look smart. Though this advice may seem superficial, it is absolutely necessary in Japan, where the packaging is as important as the contents. Try buying something as insignificant as a handkerchief and observe the time and effort the sales clerk devotes to wrapping it—no brown paper bags here. In every aspect of formal Japanese culture, the presentation or packaging is paramount.

Limit your dress to "serious" or conservative business attire. Avoid anything that could be interpreted as *pureibōi* ("playboy") or *sekushī* ("sexy") clothing.

Men: Wear dark suits, dress shirts (not necessarily white), conservative ties, black shoes (brown are too informal). Do not wear large flashy cuff links, gold necklaces, comical ties, short sleeves (considered too casual; only lower-ranking salarymen wear them).

Women: Wear charcoal gray, navy, green, or brown suits, low-heeled shoes (not over two inches). Do not wear red, pink, pastels or floral patterns (considered inappropriate in a business environment) or solid black (suggests funeral attire). Break up the black with pattern or color, with a checkered jacket, colored blouse, brooch, or scarf.

Men and women: Carry a high-quality leather briefcase and a business card holder. Keep a handkerchief with you because most bathrooms (except those in hotels) will not have paper towels. For the same reason keep tissue paper with you at all times because most bathrooms do not have toilet paper.

POSTURE

Good posture is read as a sign of intelligence and good character. A director of a U.S. multinational company had his background investigated by a potential Japanese partner solely because, during a meeting with the Japanese, the American never sat up straight and had his personal belongings and papers spread over a large area of the conference table. The Japanese wanted to know: "Is this person trustworthy?" "Are his credentials credible?" "Is he respected by his peers?" "Is he likely to be in his position long, or will he be fired or demoted because of his poor organization?"

- Keep your back straight when sitting during meetings.

- Maintain good posture at all times. Refrain from slumping, sprawling, or sitting spread-eagled. You will never see the president of a Japanese corporation slouch in a chair, much less sit on a table or lean his chair back with the front legs off the ground.

- Napping during meetings is acceptable behavior for top-ranking Japanese executives—they do it all the time. It is not, however, recommended for foreigners. Napping on the train is okay. However, make sure you nap by letting your head fall forward onto your chest. Napping with your head back and your mouth open is frowned upon. Try to keep your mouth closed unless you are speaking. Leaving it slightly open is indicative of a fool or dullard.

- Never stand with your hands behind your back, or in your pockets—especially when speaking.

- Never jiggle or tap your foot or arm nervously. This is particularly offensive to the Japanese.

- Never point directly at anyone.

- Never point to or touch someone or push something with your foot.

- Unless initiated by the other person, refrain from touching, except when shaking hands. Avoid tapping a person on the arm or giving them a clap on the shoulder.

Making Introductions

PROTOCOL

Most Japanese business settings are considerably more formal than in the U.S. Introductions are especially important and are not something to get out of the way quickly. They are essential for setting the tone of a mutually beneficial working relationship. The thoughtfulness, respect, and care that go into this phase of the partnership is the key to future business success. For your initial meeting, do the following:

* Schedule plenty of time for introductions.

* Introduce yourself to the senior or ranking Japanese person first.

* Shake hands and say, "It's nice to meet you," or use a short Japanese greeting (see "Useful Expressions," p. 164).

There is the 15-degree slight bow, the 30-degree sincere bow, the 45-degree deep bow, and the 90-degree apologizing or expressing condolences bow. You will see people bowing everywhere, even while on the telephone or standing along the pavement as a taxi or train fast disappears into the distance. As a foreigner, you should not bow, because you will most likely get it wrong. When receiving a bow from your Japanese counterpart, nod in appreciation and, at the completion of the bow, extend your hand for a handshake.

BOWING

- Present your business card.
- Make a thoughtful effort to pronounce the name. Say it twice to help keep it in your memory.
- Follow the Japanese lead and let them decide when the "real business" discussion will begin.
- Receive your Japanese counterpart's card.

SHOW RESPECT

If you don't know who the most senior Japanese person is, the behavior of the Japanese team should quickly tell you. The senior person will usually enter the room first, sit first, and be treated with deference by others. If you are still not sure, simply ask. This is not an insult. ▲ *The worst thing you can do is to not show respect to the ranking senior person, especially if you are younger. Also, do not act too familiar or casual with your Japanese counterpart's secretary. A smile and a nod are sufficient. A handshake or any touching could be considered offensive.*

INTRODUCING TEAMS

Introductions can be awkward. If teams are involved, it is best to orchestrate the introductions. First, the highest-ranking person on each team should greet one another. Others on your team should remain quiet. Second, the senior persons should introduce the members of their teams. Third, everyone should then be allowed to speak briefly with their counterparts and exchange cards with all. If there are six people on each team, this will take about 20 minutes. ▲ *Don't be impatient if a Japanese executive shows up during your meetings and all business discussions cease. You could end up chatting about non-business issues for an hour or so—this is a good sign. The Japanese are there to meet you and show interest.*

SEATING AT MEETINGS

The side of the table facing the main door is the side for the honored guest. The host should sit on the opposite side of the table with its back to the main door. Highest-ranking persons who will do little

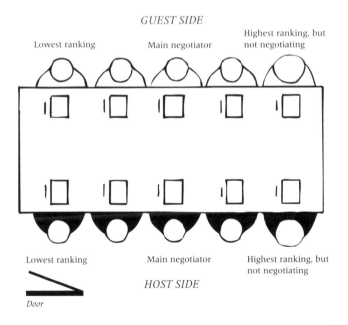

Typical seating pattern at a Japanese business meeting. The guest side is always seated toward the interior of the room as a gesture of respect.

Learn to Pronounce Japanese Names

As a foreigner you are not expected to pronounce Japanese flawlessly, but it is always appreciated if you try. Take time to pronounce your Japanese associates' names. Then ask if you are correct. To practice, review "Pronunciation," pages 162–63, and say the following Japanese names. (Pay close attention to long vowels and to the vowel **e**—it is pronounced like the **e** in "egg.")

Tanaka	Kaneko	Ōyama
Suzuki	Okabe	Oyama
Yamada	Okamoto	Kaneda
Yamamoto	Sekiguchi	Koyama
Mochizuki	Yamaguchi	Ōno
Kawada	Endō	Uchida
Nakamura	Ishii	Watanabe
Shiotani	Ōta	Kimijima
Aoki	Nobori	Ōtani
Takeshita	Kawamoto	Kawakami
Nakasone	Nishimura	Saitō
Kumakura	Shimizu	Chiba
Funabiki	Aoyama	Moriwaki
Okimoto	Doi	Ōzeki
Kanai	Ushino	Murokami
Matsumoto	Sakuma	Matsushita
Wada	Inoue	Abe
Maezawa	Yoshida	Ōtake
Yamashita	Maeda	Yokokawa

talking sit farthest from the door. The main spokespersons sit in the center of the table. If there is no ceremonial senior person, the seat farthest away from the door is not a factor in the seating. Japanese like to sit across from their Western counterparts, so seat a Japanese design engineer across from a U.S. design engineer, a Japanese marketing manager across from a U.S. marketing manager, and so on.

At less formal Japanese companies, introductions may simply be made across the table. In this case you should first stand to introduce yourself to the most senior person. For the rest of the introductions, you can either remain standing or seated while you give out your business card. Interpreters should be placed wherever they are most needed.

EXCHANGING BUSINESS CARDS

Business cards are essential for doing business in Japan. Presenting your card to someone is a universal gesture of respect that welcomes the recipient for future social and business contacts. Conversely, not doing so says to your Japanese counterpart that you do not wish to be contacted. *Running out of cards can be considered a major insult.* However, on the off chance that you do run out of cards, make copies of your last card and cut them out to card size to give with your apology. Before going to Japan, have the flip side of your card printed in Japanese (see "Making Business Cards, p. 21). This is an expected courtesy to those who do not speak English.

WHAT TO DO

- Present your card first if you are the host, lower in rank, younger, or the seller.

- Present your card to each person you are introduced to as you say, "*Dōzo yoroshiku.*" ▲ *Never deal your cards out or put them in a stack on the table for people to help themselves.*

- Present your card with both hands if at all possible. The rule of thumb is that if a Japanese has given you his card with both hands, you should receive the card with both hands and give your card with both hands. Not to return this courtesy could be viewed as an insult. In most cases, however, you will also be shaking hands or receiving a card, so presenting it with one hand is also acceptable.

- Present your card so the information is right side up for the recipient.

- Present your card with the English side up. Most Japanese will want to try to read the English.

- Shake hands. Do not try to follow the Japanese custom of bowing. A friendly nod will do.

- When receiving a card, study it. The Japanese card will usually have English on the back. Look at the presenter's title to understand his rank in the corporate hierarchy. Take time to pronounce the presenter's name out loud. Ask for assistance and correction of your pronunciation. (If the meeting seems to be moving at a rapid pace, skip this courtesy.)

- Do not give your Japanese business card to someone from another Asian country. You should have separate cards for each country you visit in Asia.

- If you mistakenly give your card to someone you have already given your card to, say you have a new phone number or a new card and that you want to make sure you pass it on.

AT THE MEETING

During the meeting, place the business cards given you by the Japanese in front of you on the table. You can line up the cards according to the seating order and refer to them as often as needed. It is much better to take your time than to rush and mispro-

You may find many people at a Japanese meeting who are there to fulfill a support role and are not necessarily part of the main event. Do not offer to introduce yourself to such support staff; always wait to be introduced, and don't be surprised if some employees are treated almost as if they are invisible. You may also see a number of women whose sole purpose is to provide tea and tidy up. Again, you do not need to acknowledge these people except perhaps to nod your head briefly when you are served tea or a snack. While this distance may make you feel awkward, it would be even more awkward for the Japanese employee whose comfortable distance has been violated.

MINDING YOUR OWN BUSINESS

nounce someone's name or get names confused. If you learn an important piece of information about a particular person, write it on that person's card (e.g., he or she likes baseball or enjoys skiing or has studied at Berkeley), but do it discreetly. This kind of information is not only important for you in the relationship-building stage but can be passed on to future players to help solidify the business relationship.

WHEN THE MEETING IS OVER

At the end of the meeting, shake the hand of the senior-ranking Japanese member first. Then either acknowledge the other members with a simple nod and a smile or take the time to shake their hands too. Finally, pick up the business cards and put them away in your briefcase. ▲ *Do not leave anyone's business card behind or throw it away in their presence. This is a grave insult.*

LANGUAGE FOR INTRODUCTIONS

INTRODUCTIONS: *GOSHŌKAI*

Give the following greeting the first time you are introduced to someone.

Corporate Departments

理事会	*rijikai*	board of directors
総務	*sōmu*	general administration
経理	*keiri*	accounting
製造	*seizō*	manufacturing
品質管理	*hinshitsu kanri*	quality control
営業	*eigyō*	sales
販売	*hanbai*	marketing
宣伝	*senden*	promotion
開発	*kaihatsu*	development
財務	*zaimu*	financial affairs
人事	*jinji*	personnel

Corporate Titles

会長	*kaichō*	chairman
副会長	*fukukaichō*	vice-chairman
社長	*shachō*	president (CEO)
副社長	*fukushachō*	executive vice president
専務取締役	*senmu torishimariyaku*	senior managing director
常務取締役	*jōmu torishimariyaku*	managing director
取締役	*torishimariyaku*	director
支店長	*shitenchō*	branch manager
部長	*buchō*	department head
次長	*jichō*	assistant general manager
課長	*kachō*	section manager or head
課長補佐	*kachō hosa*	assistant section manager
係長	*kakarichō*	group chief
部員、課員	*buin, kain*	staff member

First say:

Hajimemashite.   Nice to meet you.

Then say:

[YOUR NAME] **desu.**   I am [YOUR NAME].
Dōzo yoroshiku.   I'm indebted./ It's a pleasure.
                      [lit., "Please do for me."]

Now offer your card, shake hands, and continue on in English. ▲ *If you do not have time to practice your greeting in Japanese, it is best to introduce yourself in English and add "**Dōzo yoroshiku**" ("It's a pleasure") at the end. This phrase will go a long way toward showing that you have taken time to learn an important greeting.*

HONORIFIC ADDRESSES

Always use your Japanese counterparts' last names when referring to them, with either the English prefix "Mr.," "Mrs.," or "Ms." or with the Japanese suffix **-san**, as in "Mr. Tanaka" or "Tanaka-**san**." *Never* refer to "Mr. Tanaka-**san**" and *never* use the honorific -**san** with your own name. If a Japanese business contact has asked you to use his first name, it is best to do so only in informal settings. Informally, or in one-on-one situations, you could address Hideo Yamaguchi as "Hideo"; in formal situations such as customer meetings or negotiations, address him as "Mr. Yamaguchi."

In most cases, it would be best to refer to Mr. Tanaka as "Director Tanaka" or "Mr. Tanaka" rather than using the Japanese "Tanaka-**san**." This is because many senior Japanese prefer name plus title, as in "Tanaka-**buchō**."

Strategies
for
Meetings

TOPICS OF CONVERSATION

FORMAL SETTINGS

Questions you can expect at an initial meeting *before* business talks begin:

> "How was your flight?"
>
> "Is this your first time in Japan?"
>
> "What are your travel plans for this trip?"

Questions you can expect at an initial meeting *after* business discussion begins:

> "How many plants does your company have in the U.S.?"

"Where are your subsidiaries?"

"How many employees does your company have worldwide?"

"What are your company's future plans for the Japanese market?"

Before you begin a *formal* presentation, you should:

- State your full name and title and where you fit into your company's organization and the team you came with.

- Explain your area of expertise—this is a good time to establish your credibility. If you have been with your company only a few years, emphasize your years of experience in the field.

INFORMAL SETTINGS

In an initial *informal* setting such as a business lunch or dinner, or over drinks, you may be asked the following questions:

"What is your background?"—meaning your educational background.

"What is your first impression of Japan?"

"Do you like Japanese food?"—if there is a particular food you do not like, this is the time to say something like, "I enjoy tempura and sukiyaki very much, but I don't like to eat **sashimi** [raw fish]."

"Can you use chopsticks?"

"How many children do you have?"

"Have you been to Japan before?"

"What are your hobbies?"

"What is your favorite Japanese baseball player?"

ACCEPTABLE TOPICS OF CONVERSATION

You can also volunteer information on the following subjects:

- your first impressions of Japan (something complimentary is required)

- your previous experiences in Japan, which should be positive or at least humorous

- your interest in Japanese culture—sumo wrestling, Japanese baseball, traditional theater (Noh, Kabuki), the Tokyo symphony, Japanese hot springs, traditional festivals, etc.

- your home town

- their hobbies and yours

- travel experiences in general

TABOO TOPICS OF CONVERSATION

Keep in mind that it is very easy to let the conversation be one-sided. You should also ask questions about your Japanese host. Avoid the following subjects:

- the role of the emperor in Japanese society, and any negative remarks about members of the royal family

- politics in general

- Japan-Korea relations

- World War II

- trade friction

- wives, even if a Japanese man inquires about yours (As a rule, in a business context, Japanese men do not talk about their wives and would feel uncomfortable if the subject were brought up. An exception to this rule is that if a man says something about his own wife first you know it is a comfortable subject for him.)

Once you get to know your Japanese counterpart these subjects will no longer be off limits, but as a foreigner you should still be politely cautious.

STEREOTYPES TO AVOID

Do not refer to Japanese as Asian or Oriental. Eliminate these words from your vocabulary. No one likes to be classified under the heading of a collective noun. Furthermore, this will make you look insensitive and uneducated. Instead, refer to individuals specifically as Chinese, Japanese, Korean, Vietnamese, etc. If you must refer to all people in the region, use "our vendors in the Pacific hemisphere."

Don't use the term "Far East." Far from whom? This will be interpreted as an ethnocentric remark and will not help open channels of informal conversation.

You should avoid discussing the conditions of the Ainu (Japan's aboriginal population in Hokkaido, who have largely mixed with Japanese) and the Korean and Chinese populations in Japan.

IMPROVING COMMUNICATION

Modify your communication style to match a formal occasion: be emotionally restrained, use polite language, and show deference to seniors and those in positions of authority.

- Ask questions that open the lines of communication with the sometimes reticent Japanese. For difficulties to surface, you need to provide the opportunity. For example, even when there seems to be agreement on the deadline, ask, "What difficulties do you see in making this deadline?" or "What can I do to help you out with this?" Then you will get the real answer.

- Don't allow yourself to be the only topic of conversation.

- Do not react with impatience to seemingly unorganized meetings and random questions.

- Listen more and talk less. The Japanese perception of Americans is that they talk all the time.

- Never use in-house interpreters supplied by the client. Take your own—either from your subsidiary or hired from a professional agency (see "Using an Interpreter," p. 100).

- Tone down your gestures and facial expressions.

- Don't worry if the Japanese avoid eye contact when you are talking. This doesn't mean that your presentation is bombing.

- Don't boast.

- Don't oversell yourself or your company.

- Don't claim to have more responsibility than you do. This will surely backfire and cost you your credibility. (Always err in the direction of modesty.)

- Watch out for the green tea you will always be offered. It contains a lot of caffeine and can jangle your nerves.

- Warning: Japanese often drink iced coffee. It may look like a cola, but it won't taste like one. The tiny pitcher of clear liquid that comes with iced coffee and tea is sugar syrup.

- Don't schedule too much late-night business entertainment. Get plenty of rest. The Japanese may try to send in fresh troops for an afternoon meeting.

- Between sessions, write informal summaries and give them to your counterpart to look over for you. Ask to meet over coffee or drinks before the next session to informally discuss your understanding.

- Don't try to act too Japanese.

CROSS-CULTURAL COMMUNICATION TIPS

When addressing a Japanese person, slow down your speed of delivery a bit but not to the point of sounding condescending. Being spoken to too fast is the number one complaint from Japanese business people. Don't mumble or slur your words. In addition:

- Don't speak pidgin English or delete articles such as "a," "the," and "and" from your own speech.

- Don't finish sentences for a Japanese, non-native speaker.

- Don't automatically fill silences. Non-native speakers need more time than you do.

- Remember to include the non-native speaker in your group conversation.

- When repetition is requested, repeat exactly what you just said.

- Summarize and rephrase often.

- Don't increase the volume of your speech. Loud doesn't help.

- Idioms can be hard to avoid, so take time to explain them.

- Use clarifying phrases to probe for understanding: "Please explain further" or "Please give more background information on _____."

- Don't use humor in a formal business setting. Jokes don't translate well across cultures and show a lack of seriousness and respect in a formal business setting in Japan.

- Don't use swear words.

- Avoid irony or sarcasm. It will most likely be misunderstood.

- Don't judge a person's intelligence based on his/her English-language ability.

- Speaking in a foreign language can be very tiring. Be sure to express your appreciation for the efforts the Japanese are making to speak English to you.

- Allow the Japanese to speak among themselves. This will increase the ease of discussion and input from the Japanese side.

- Do make an effort to allow for input from non-native English participants. Native English speakers need to give non-native speakers time for processing.

- Call on people by name for input. For the most part, only valuable, pertinent information will be volunteered by Japanese employees. The informal observations and personal remarks common in the West are usually absent from business meetings in Japan.

▲ *Take time up front to learn each participant's name and how to pronounce it. This will set the tone for true cross-cultural participation.*

USING AN INTERPRETER

Always hire your own interpreter. Either your subsidiary will provide one, or you can make arrangements through the business center at your hotel. The cost of a professional consecutive interpreter runs anywhere from ¥60,000 to ¥90,000 per day.

SIMULTANEOUS VS. CONSECUTIVE INTERPRETERS

You have a choice whether you want a simultaneous interpreter to speak as you are speaking, or a consecutive interpreter to speak during pauses you insert into your speech. Simultaneous interpreting allows you to make a more natural presentation, but there are few interpreters who excel at it, and those that do are *very* expensive. In most cases, a consecutive interpreter will suffice.

GUIDELINES

- Schedule at least one hour to talk with your interpreter before the meeting to discuss your objectives, explain key words, and establish a rapport. If consecutive interpreting, ask how often you should pause during your speech for smooth, comfortable interpreting. If confidentiality is important, have the interpreter sign a non-disclosure agreement.

- Calculate that your presentation will be about one and a half times its English-language length when it is consecutively interpreted.

- Some of your audience will want to try to listen to you rather than the interpreter. As a courtesy, speak slowly but naturally.

- Initially speak about three or four sentences at a time and then pause for the consecutive interpreter. Once your presentation is underway, you can speak in longer thought groups. But be sure to check with your interpreter during a break to see if you need to slow down or speed up. If you have a prepared script you have given the interpreter beforehand, you can speak for a longer time before pausing for interpretation.

- Do not be surprised if the interpreter translates what seems to be a lengthy segment from only a few English sentences, or vice versa. Japanese and English are very different languages. In order to make your message sound natural, the interpreter will make many adjustments in phrasing.

- If the interpreter is having difficulty with a word or phrase, pause and take the time to clarify.

- If only one interpreter is being used, take a 10-minute break every hour.

- Look at the person you are speaking to. Act as if the interpreter doesn't exist. Say, "What are your considerations?"—not "What are her/his considerations?" But do occasionally acknowledge the interpreter as a courtesy.

- Take particular care when discussing numbers. Japanese and English have different numerical systems and it is easy to make mistakes when going back and forth between the two languages. Write out numbers larger than 10,000.

BUSINESS IN MOTION

SEATING IN VEHICLES

Seating order depends on the mode of transportation (car, train, plane). There are, however, exceptions. For example, women wearing kimono and overweight people may prefer to get into the car last. Some people prefer to sit by the aisle in an airplane so they can enter and exit their seats easily. In a crowded train, seating order can be disregarded, though if seating is scarce, the senior executive, then older persons, are offered seats first.

SEEING SOMEONE OFF

Cordial good-byes last after the meeting breaks up and the guest's team leaves the meeting room. At the very least, guests are escorted to the elevator of the host's building, in which case the host's team lines up outside the elevator to say good-bye until the door closes. When seeing someone off in a car or train, the host's side waits until the car or train has left and can no longer be seen.

Direction of travel

① ② Salesman ③ ④

TOP: *Seating order when riding on a train. Seniority or corporate rank is indicated by number.* RIGHT: *Seating order when riding on an airplane.*

Salesman

③ ② ① Window side

TOP: *Seating pattern when using a taxi.* BOTTOM: *Seating pattern when a staff member is driving. If the driver is a very junior employee, the top seating is more appropriate.*

RESOLVING CONFLICTS

Approach difficult situations through informal discussion. Don't appear agitated or overly anxious in front of the Japanese.

- Don't be confrontational.

- Don't spell out every last detail. Leave room for the other party to maneuver and show good intentions. (Even if you have to wait a day or two, the wait is far better than taking the risk of damaging the relationship.)

- If things are not going well, drop the discussion and continue it at a later time.

- Always listen first.

- Present your opinion or position calmly, clearly, and often. Repetition is your strongest tool.

- Don't push for decisions. The person you are talking to is not necessarily the real decision maker.

- If you feel you have spoken too strongly, this is a good time to socialize with the Japanese after work. But don't discuss the problem. Use the opportunity to reestablish the relationship.

- If all else fails, or if you feel that the differences between you and the Japanese side are too great and too incomprehensible, ask a mutual acquaintance to intercede on your behalf and find out what's wrong. Then you are in a position to know whether you should apologize or simply leave things alone. ▲ *If you feel the problem is your responsibility, the best course of action is to apologize through a third party and never mention the issue again.*

Business Communications *Kuizu*

What is the appropriate response in each situation?

1. When introducing yourself to Japanese businessperson:
   (a) Shake hands, say something light or funny, and get down to business. (b) Bow at a 45° angle and introduce yourself in Japanese. (c) Shake hands, bow, and introduce yourself in Japanese. (d) Formally shake hands, exchange business cards, and state that it is a pleasure to make his/her acquaintance.

2. When giving your business card to a Japanese:
   (a) Offer it with both hands. (b) Offer it to the most junior person first. (c) Offer it to the most senior person first. (d) When meeting someone in a more senior position, offer your business card only after receiving his/hers. (e) Upon receiving someone's card, pay attention to the name and title and attempt to pronounce the name correctly. (f) a, c, d, and e. (g) b, d, and e.

3. It is considered rude to:
   (a) Write on someone's business card. (b) Place the business cards on the table and refer to them as you speak. (c) Leave the cards behind when you leave the meeting room. (d) Discreetly toss the business cards you don't need into the wastebasket as you exit the meeting room. (e) Put someone's card in your rear pocket and sit down. (f) c, d, and e. (g) All of the above.

4. When giving a presentation to a Japanese audience:
   (a) Give the entire speech in Japanese. (b) Look only at the most senior-ranking person on the Japanese side. (c) Speak slowly but naturally; avoid idioms, slang idiomatic expressions, and long complex sentences. (d) Gesture to make your points, e.g., show three fingers when you say, "I have three points I wish to make." (e) All of the above.

5. When you hear a "yes" from the Japanese side, it means:
(a) They agree. (b) They would like to agree. (c) They have heard your request. (d) They have heard your request and understand it. (e) They are trying to throw you off by saying yes and then doing nothing. (f) They are trying to buy time. (g) Possibly all of the above.

6. In the initial stages of business relations, it is a good idea to:
(a) Call your Japanese counterparts by their last names. (b) Allow for general questions and answers as a way of establishing credibility and trust. (c) Not rush the agenda. (d) Not present yourself as someone who has more decision-making power than you actually have. (e) All of the above.

7. Getting the "silent treatment" means the Japanese are:
(a) Seriously considering what you said. (b) Upset with what you said and are trying to tell you so. (c) Taking a moment to rest. (d) Aware that it drives you crazy and want to throw you off. (e) a, b, and c. (f) Possibly all of the above.

8. In a difficult situation, one thing you should not do is:
(a) Resort to aggressive displays of impatience and anger. (b) Be non-confrontational. (c) Keep your explanations short and simple. (d) Say you are not sure you understand and ask questions. (e) Say how you truly feel.

9. The best way to resolve interpersonal difficulties is :
(a) Have a one-on-one, heart-to-heart discussion. (b) Write a letter explaining the way you see the issue. (c) Use a third party to intercede on your behalf. (d) Call and talk about the problem on the telephone. (e) Give an expensive or prestigious gift.

ANSWERS
1-d. 2-f. 3-f. 4-c. 5-g. 6-e. 7-f. 8-a. 9-c then a.

LANGUAGE FOR BUSINESS MEETINGS

The following are useful phrases to incorporate into your meetings in Japan. Say the phrase, and then continue speaking in English. No one will think you are fluent in Japanese, but your efforts will be appreciated.

THANK YOUS

Upon meeting again:

> *Kono aida wa dōmo.*
> Thank you for the other day/occasion.

Upon leaving your hosts before leaving the country:

> *Iro iro dōmo arigatō gozaimasu.*
> Thank you for all you have done.

When someone does you a big favor:

> *Taihen deshita ne. Dōmo iroiro sumimasen deshita.*
> That was a lot to ask. Thank you for everything. (I'm sorry to have inconvenienced you.)

Upon receiving a gift or a report you requested:

> [OBJECT] *wa dōmo arigatō gozaimasu.*
> Thank you very much for the [OBJECT].

After someone took the time to help you:

> *Taihen isogashii tokoro, dōmo osewa ni narimashita.*
> Thank you for taking time to help me when you are so busy. (I am in your debt.)

Meeting Concluding and Follow-up

Summaries: When concluding a cross-cultural meeting, the one thing you must do is summarize the agreement and action items in real time. There are several ways to do this. If you have a white board that also copies, write out the agreement and/or action items on the white board, and when everyone is satisfied and has initialed it, copy the board and hand everyone in the room their own copy. This will be the minutes of the meeting and will save countless hours of clarifying what went on in the meeting through e-mail, faxes, or phone conversations. If a white board is not available, put up a blank transparency and do the same.

Leave-behinds: Leave a copy of all the information on your presentation for each of the Japanese team so they can go over it after you have left.

Follow-up meetings: If you plan to remain in Japan for a few more days, suggest that small or one-on-one post-meeting sessions be scheduled with the appropriate Japanese principals to go over the details of your presentation.

Thank yous: Always telephone to thank your Japanese hosts for taking time to arrange and attend the meeting. You can then follow up your call with an e-mail to reiterate the main points of the meeting or clarify points you did not understand.

Upon meeting someone who took you out for dinner the night before:

> *Kinō no yoru wa dōmo arigatō gozaimasu. Totemo tanoshikatta desu.*
> Thank you for last night. It was very enjoyable.

APOLOGIES

Upon leaving a meeting for a few minutes:

> **Sumimasen. Chotto shitsurei shimasu.**
> Excuse me for a moment.

Upon leaving a meeting or work early:

> **Sumimasen. Shitsurei shimasu.**
> Excuse me. (I am being rude.)

You just found out that you had misunderstood something:

> **Dōmo kono aida wa sumimasen deshita. Watashi wa wakarimasen deshita ga. . . .** [continue in English]
> Excuse me for the other day. I did not understand. . . .

You are having a hard time understanding things:

> **Mada iroiro wakarimasen. Sumimasen.**
> I still don't understand a great many things. I'm sorry. (Excuse me.)

Phone, Fax, and E-mail

PUTTING THE PHONE TO WORK

Japanese complain about and sometimes even try to avoid people who are long-winded on the telephone. It is tiring for a non-native speaker to handle English conversations on the phone. Prepare your questions in advance so they are clear and concise. This will avoid frustration on both sides. Here are some suggestions:

- Speak slowly but naturally.

- For a critical business matter, particularly when numbers are involved, send information ahead of time by fax or e-mail and then follow up with a phone call.

- Keep it short, but don't skip being personal. Relationships also need to be maintained by phone.

- Don't ask "yes/no" questions for clarification. Instead, ask

Sample Fax and E-mail Format

Below is a recommended format for fax transmissions and e-mail to a Japanese company.

Header Info:

> DATE: (spell out the month; don't use all numbers)
> TO: *Name, title, and department* (if you know it)
> CC: *Names of anyone you are copying the e-mail or fax to, and their company*
> FROM: *Your full name*
> RE: *Subject*
> PGS: *Total number of pages* (for faxes only, of course)

"Wet stuff": Acknowledgments, thank yous, or non-business chit-chat, e.g.:

> "We received your shipment this morning."
> "Thank you for your reply of December 10."
> "I appreciate your taking time to meet with me yesterday."
> "I hope you are enjoying the holidays."

Apology: If needed, e.g.:

> "Please accept my apology for not getting back to you sooner."
> "I am sorry to have missed you last time you were in Dallas."

"what," "where," when," "why," and "who" questions. This will give you information rather than just a vague yes or no response.

• Don't expect to make major decisions over the phone. Your Japanese contact will most likely want to make important commitments in writing.

Text. Use an outline form or number your points. Writing this way is best because (1) it cuts down on unnecessary verbiage, (2) you clarify your ideas by putting the topic sentence first followed by supporting information, (3) your Japanese counterparts can clearly refer to each issue by number in their response, and (4) you can find each issue by number if you need to follow up.

Conclusion. Make a short statement to wrap up what you have written, make a request for a response, or communicate what you plan to do next, e.g.:

> "I believe this covers all the points we discussed during our Tuesday meeting."
>
> "I will contact you at 9 AM your time on Thursday during our regular phone meeting. If you have any questions about the above, I would be happy to answer them at that time."
>
> "Please let us know your views on these points."
>
> "We look forward to hearing from you about this matter at your earliest convenience."
>
> "I look forward to seeing you in Tokyo next month."

▲ *If you have to send a fax or e-mail again, do not rewrite it but simply put "Re-send" or "Second Request" on the original's Subject line and send it again. Rewriting will possibly cause your Japanese counterparts to retranslate it to see if you are saying something different.*

- When repetition is requested, repeat exactly what you just said.
- If you don't understand, say so, and indicate you will call back to discuss the matter at a later date.

▲ *Anytime you can send a template of the information you are requesting it will help out your Japanese counterpart and speed the information flow.*

Phone Tips

As a rule, the written English of most non-native speakers is better than the spoken. Therefore, a very successful strategy is a three-step approach for critical issues:

1. Send a written message so that your Japanese team member can understand ahead of time the intent and some specifics that are to be discussed.

2. Speak by phone so that a great deal of non-formal communication can take place.

3. Summarize, if needed, the phone discussion points in written form.

LANGUAGE FOR THE PHONE

When you call a Japanese company, you can never be sure that the person who picks up the phone on the other end speaks English. If you learn the few phrases here and follow the above common-sense phone tips, you should be able to get through to the person you want to speak with.

The person on the other end will generally answer the phone by giving the name of the company, just as in the U.S. You should say:

> *Moshi moshi. Kochira wa* [YOUR NAME] *desu*. [NAME OF PERSON]-*san wa irasshaimasu ka?*
> Hello. My name is [YOUR NAME]. Is Mr./Ms.[NAME OF PERSON] there?

The person at the company will then probably say one of the following phrases:

Hai, shōshō omachi kudasai.
Yes, just a moment please.

Sumimasen, ima gaishutsu shite orimasu.
I'm sorry, he/she is out of the office right now.

Sumimasen, mō ichido onegaishimasu.
Excuse me, please repeat what you just said.

If the person you want is not there, you can say:

Dōmo arigato gozaimasu. Mata odenwa shimasu.
Thank you very much. I will call again.

Or you can say:

Itsugoro mata odenwa shitara yoroshii deshō ka?
When would be a good time to call back?

If you do not understand, say:

*Sumimasen ga. Nihongo ga wakarimasen. Eigo ga hanaseru
hito onegai dekimasen ka?*
I'm sorry, I don't understand Japanese. Could I please request
someone who speaks English?

Socializing

BUSINESS AFTER HOURS

FOR THE BUSINESSMAN

After-hours entertainment is obligatory. It can be pleasant if you relax, forget your fatigue, and allow the evening to unfold. This is time to enjoy the personal side of Japanese business and get to know your associates better. Given that you must participate in the evening's merriment, you should know the good news—you are not required to drink. If you don't drink, you have three options. (1) You can accept a drink and sip it all evening. The danger of this strategy is that Japanese protocol demands that everyone pour drinks for you, so as soon as you have taken a few sips someone will want to fill up your glass. If you don't pay attention, you can easily sip yourself into a state of intoxication. (2) You can accept the hospitality and then don't touch your drink. (3) You can order a non-alcoholic beverage and explain that you don't drink. Whichever option you choose, remember to remain politely informal throughout the evening. Japanese can let their hair down and seem unembarrassed by activities such as singing in public, acting inebriated, or even behaving in a silly or risque manner. These behaviors, which can cause anxiety for Westerners, are acceptable for Japanese as long as they are not overly disgusting or disruptive. The best way to handle a situation like this, if it becomes uncomfortable for you, is to keep your tact intact. There are some unique entertainments, however, that you may be grateful to have been warned about: karaoke bars, hostess bars, and elevator girls.

Karaoke Bars

When it comes to drinking, you can choose to drink or not, but when it comes to singing, you must sing! What will you sing? Try "Danny Boy," "I Left My Heart in San Francisco," "My Way," or any Beatles or John Denver song. Practice one on your own until you feel comfortable singing it. If you want to be truly bold, try a Frank Sinatra or Elvis impersonation. These are the standards anywhere in Japan, though you may be surprised to find that some bars have a very up-to-date selection of current U.S. pop music to choose from. Don't worry about your performance. The electronics systems and state-of-the-art chambers are uniformly first-class, helping even the most mediocre singers sound like pros. Sounding great is not the point. The point is to enjoy yourself and, at times, let others enjoy your embarrassment.

Hostess Bars

Each customers gets a personal "hostess" at these very expensive bars. The hostess is assigned to you and you only. She is not a prostitute. Her role is to help you relax and enjoy the evening. She may

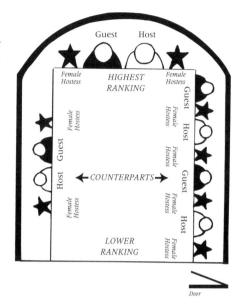

Typical seating pattern at a hostess bar. Higher ranking people sit toward the rear of the room, and host and guest counterparts sit next to and across from each other to facilitate conversation.

Guest   Host

Female Hostess   HIGHEST RANKING   Female Hostess

Female Hostess   Guest

Female Hostess   Host

Guest   Female Hostess

Host   ←COUNTERPARTS→   Female Hostess   Guest

Female Hostess   Host

Female Hostess

LOWER RANKING   Female Hostess

Door

occasionally speak English, ask you questions through your Japanese hosts about your work, and encourage you to talk, drink, and sing. Japanese will take foreigners to hostess bars because they think this will impress you. If this is not your style, accept the first time and, afterward, tell your host you feel privileged to have had the experience and offer your thanks for a very enjoyable evening. Then suggest that next time you go to a quieter place—where there are no hostesses—so you can talk together more easily. It is all right to let your preferences be known.

Elevator Girls

These are not your ordinary, uniformed elevator girls who wave you onto department store elevators and bow as the door closes. The "elevator girls" you need to know about are the ones who ride the hotel elevators, watch where you go, and end up in your room, on your bed. She may say something like, "Let's practice English a little." But it's not English she wants to practice. She wants to see how easy it will be to get you to part with your cash. Simply asking her to leave does not always work. The quickest, surest way to get her out of your room is to say that you will call security if she doesn't leave. She will bother you no more.

FOR THE BUSINESSWOMAN

The businesswoman also needs to participate in business after hours, but not at the bars, hostess bars, and clubs. You may be invited to go but, unless your host insists, it is appreciated if you decline. These are environments dedicated solely to serving the male, and you may not feel comfortable or welcome. Women can instead schedule lunches or coffee breaks at nearby coffee shops or early dinners. If you are unfamiliar with the city, ask that dinner be at your hotel or nearby so that you can easily bow out after the meal. The advantage of being a woman is that you can get a good night's sleep and be ready to go the next day while your male colleagues won't be in quite the same shape. ▲ *If you follow these guidelines, (1) you will project a professional image, which is very important in Japan, and (2) you will raise the comfort level of the Japanese people who will be working with you. Once you know your Japanese counterparts, you can relax these boundaries.*

BELIEVE IT OR NOT QUESTIONS—AND POSSIBLE ANSWERS

The rules of etiquette in informal, late-night settings in Japan are different from those during the day. While you can say almost anything while socializing and it will not be brought up the next day, as a foreigner you should be more circumspect than your Japanese counterparts, who may ask you questions of an extremely personal nature. Such questions are not usually intended to be rude or offensive. They may simply represent curiosity about the outside world or foreign lifestyles. Japanese also believe that Westerners are more open about intimate topics and don't mind discussing them. Sometimes, however, the questions *are* out of line. It is up to you to set the limits. Typical questions:

- How much money do you make?
- How old are you?
- Are you married?
- How many times have you been married?
- Why aren't you married?
- How many children do you have?
- What do you think of Japanese men/women?
- How is it that your husband lets you travel?
- Do you like sexy jokes?

If you want to politely stop this line of questioning, make your answer vague and change the subject. When asked, "How much money do you make?" say, with a smile, "Much more than I am worth." When asked, "Do you like sexy jokes," women especially should be more direct and say, "No!" As a woman, if you don't stop the attempt at sexual dialogue at the onset, a lot more could follow, and it will damage your effectiveness in the business relationship.

ETIQUETTE

Let the Japanese direct you to your seat. Seating is important both in Japanese business and social environments. Your hosts may feel

Food display of the sort you might be served at a traditional Japanese-style dinner. Always place the chopsticks on the chopsticks holder when they are not in use.

Tea

Grilled food

Sashimi

Rice

Dipping sauce

Chopsticks

Soup

uncomfortable if you sit next to someone who is too junior or in a seat toward the door (the guest usually sits toward the interior of the room).

- Let your host order for you. Accepting this kind of hospitality is seen as a gracious act.

- Stay in step with everyone. As best you can, watch what the Japanese do and follow their lead. Japanese restaurants serve food when it is ready; if your meal arrives first your host likely will insist that you begin. It is okay to do so.

- Do not pour your own tea, beer, sake, or other drinks. You and your hosts will take turns pouring for each other.

- At the beginning of the evening, when the first drinks are poured, do not begin to drink until everyone has been served. Then glasses are raised for a toast, when everyone says "*Kanpai!*" ("bottoms up").

- If you don't drink alcohol, you can accept a drink anyway and nurse it for the entire evening.

- When someone pours for you, lift your glass with both hands toward the pourer. If it is awkward to do so, simply hold the glass without lifting it. If you have had enough, keep lifting your

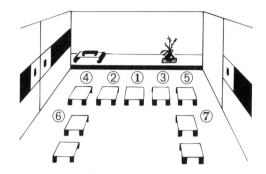

Typical seating pattern at a formal Japanese-style dinner. The higher-ranking people sit toward the displays at the back of the room.

glass or cup away from the pourer so that it is difficult to fill. This will encourage a laugh, and give others the message that you don't want to drink any more.

- When eating Japanese-style cuisine:

    do not pour soy sauce on the rice to "flavor" it (you can pour it on anything else)

    if your chopsticks have splinters, don't scrape them together at the table; you can do this discreetly under the table, or ask for another pair

    never point your chopsticks at anyone or poise them over the communal food bowl looking for tasty morsels

    do not use the end of the chopsticks that go in your mouth to take food from a communal bowl; instead, turn the chopsticks around and pick up food with the other end

    remove the lids from your dishes and place them upside down on the table or next to the tray; when finished, put them back on the bowls in the original position.

    Japanese diners will often take a sip or two of miso soup before they eat their rice; if you follow suit and dip your chopsticks into the soup for a morsel, your rice won't stick to them

leave some food in your bowl to show you are not still hungry

don't pierce food with your chopsticks; if the piece of food is too big, pick up the whole piece, bite off a portion, and return the rest to the plate

for fish, you can easily break off a small piece before lifting it to your mouth; if the fish has bones, press along the backbone with your chopsticks; this will loosen the meat from the bone

don't stick your chopsticks upright into the rice; this is a gesture used at Buddhist funeral ceremonies.

- Remember that what you say or what you are told while drinking is not to be brought up the next day in a formal business setting (with the exception of important information you are meant to know, which should be revealed cautiously and in private, if possible).

- If you are treating the Japanese, make all the arrangements for paying ahead of time, out of sight of your guests.

- Never put your feet on the furniture or expose the bottom of your shoe (as would happen when you sit with the ankle of one leg crossed over the knee of another). Keeping your legs together and feet flat on the floor is the safest way to sit in a chair. This applies at the office as well.

IN THE HOME

Japanese generally think that their living spaces are too small and humble to receive guests, so foreigners are rarely invited to visit a private home. If you are lucky enough to receive an invitation, the following will help you avoid embarrassing faux pas.

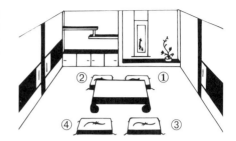

Typical seating pattern at a small, informal Japanese-style dinner. The higher-ranking people (or guests) sit toward the displays at the back of the room.

- Always take along a gift of something edible—a box of candy, some small cakes, some fruit, or a bottle of imported wine or scotch. You can purchase such gifts in department store food sections, and it is perfectly acceptable to present them in department store wrappings. Do not be surprised, however, if your host does not open your gift while you are there. (See "How to Give and Receive Gifts," pp. 17–19).

- Remove and leave your shoes in the entranceway, with the toes pointing toward the door. Your host may take them from you to place in a shoe box to retrieve on your way out.

- House slippers may be offered to you at the door. Wear them while walking on hardwood floors, but take them off before entering tatami-matted rooms. Only bare or stocking feet should touch tatami.

- Toilet slippers are provided for the toilet only. Do not wear them anywhere except the toilet area.

- The formal posture for sitting on the floor is with your back straight and both legs folded under you. You are not, however, expected to sit this way as it is very uncomfortable, even for the Japanese. Instead, men can cross their legs, and women can tuck their legs to one side.

- Do not leave the room you have been ushered into to take a look around unless invited to do so. If you need to use the bathroom, ask the host/hostess and let them lead you there or point the way.

- Do not offer to assist in serving dinner or clearing away dishes from the table.

- After placing the food on the table, the host will expect you to start first. *Itadakimasu* (lit., "I humbly receive") is the standard expression used before you begin your meal, and *Gochisōsama deshita* ("Thank you for the repast") is said when you have finished your meal, and again when leaving.

- In conversation, your host may show his private face by speaking negatively about family or job, or expressing personal concerns. If you think he is fishing for a compliment, you may want to provide one. If what he says seems uncomfortably personal, acknowledge him with an "I understand how it must be" and then politely change the subject.

- Express your appreciation for the evening as you leave (you can repeatthe phrase *Gochisōsama deshita* at this time to thank your host again for the meal). If you meet your host the next day at the office, thank him politely once more. Do not on any account, however, mention anything personal that was said the evening before.

LANGUAGE FOR SOCIALIZING

On the following page are some useful phrases you can use to make conversation or interject into your speech. Say the phrase, and then continue on speaking in English.

Kore wa oishii desu.
This is delicious.

Kore wa nan desu ka?
What is this?

Mō ippon nomimashō.
Let's drink another bottle (of beer, sake, or soda).

Endō-san wa kodomo ga imasu ka?
Mr. Endō, do you have any children?

Shashin ga arimasu ka?
Do you have any photos?

"Hobby" wa nan desu ka?
What are your hobbies?

Kyō wa tsukaremashita ne!
Today was tiring, wasn't it!

Kyō wa totemo tanoshikatta desu.
Today was very enjoyable.

Kyō, iroiro arigatō gozaimashita.
Thank you very much for everything you did today.

Kondo wa Amerika ni kite kudasai.
Next time (you) come to America.

Amerika de nani ka shitai koto ga arimasu ka?
Is there something you wish to do in America?

Totemo subarashikatta desu. Dōmo arigatō gozaimashita.
Thank you for a wonderful time.

Mata ashita.
See you tomorrow.

THE PHONE SYSTEM

PUBLIC PHONES

Telecommunicating in Japan is easy and reliable. Public phones are everywhere and are cheaper (¥10 for 3 minutes for local calls) than calling from your hotel. Your hotel will have a fax machine. Long-distance rates are lower at night and on weekends and holidays.

Public telephones can come in almost any color. As a general rule, green phones take telephone cards; most also take ¥10 and ¥100 coins (if the call does not go through, they return unused coins, but there is no change back for ¥100 coins). Yellow phones also accept ¥10 and ¥100 coins. Red phones accept only ¥10 coins. Pink phones, usually found at restaurants and shops, are used the same way as green phones; some even accept telephone cards. Upscale shops use cordless pay phones. Dark blue phones take coins and credit cards, and gray phones, with monitor screens that give instructions in Japanese and English, take coins and cards and can be used for international calls. The 001-1C Global Phone used for overseas calls can be accessed with a 001-1C Global Card in one of four denominations: ¥1,000, ¥2,000, ¥3,000, or ¥5,000, all of which include a 10% bonus on top of their units.

TELEPHONE CARDS

Prepaid telephone cards, decorated with photos, pictures, or logos, are magnetically encoded with phone units, each one representing ¥10 worth of phone time. Insert them in hotel phones and green public telephones, and the phone units will be deducted from your cards as you speak. When your card is depleted, buy a new one. Cards are available in units of 50 (¥500) and 105 (¥1,000), and can be purchased at phone-card vending machines, hotels, convenience stores, train station kiosks, and tobacco shops. If you think you will use public telephones frequently, purchase a telephone card so you won't have to keep feeding coins into the telephone while talking.

USEFUL NUMBERS

PHONE ASSISTANCE IN ENGLISH

English-speaking operators are available for questions and assistance. Call toll free **(0120) 364-463** (9 AM to 5 PM, weekdays).

DIRECTORY ASSISTANCE

Dial **104** on an NTT public phone and, speaking slowly and clearly, ask for the domestic number you need. The cost is ¥30 per inquiry. Dial **106** for credit card or collect calls.

DOMESTIC CALLS FROM PUBLIC PHONES

Use any phone to place a local or domestic long-distance direct call. Pick up the receiver and insert a telephone card or coin. When you hear the dial tone, place your call. When placing an intercity call, the number must start with the two- or three-digit area code beginning with zero. (When you are calling from outside Japan, the zero is dropped.) Local codes follow, and then subscribers' numbers:

Tokyo	**(03)** (Tokyo Area Code)	
	+ 3456 (Local Code)	
	+ 7890 (Subscriber's Number)	
Yokohama	**(045)**	
Osaka	**(066**)	
Nagoya	**(052)**	
Kyoto	**(075**)	
Kobe	**(078**)	
Hiroshima	**(082)**	
Fukuoka	**(092)**	
Sapporo	**(011**)	

A beep signals when your money is used up, so have another card or some change ready or the phone will cut you off abruptly.

INTERNATIONAL CALLS

To dial direct, use a green public phone with a gold front plate or an

"International & Domestic Card/Coin Telephone" sticker on the front, or a large gray telephone. These are available in the airports and business centers of major cities. The calls will be cheaper than from the hotel, where surcharges are applied. KDD (the main phone company in Japan) has a "KDD Credit Phone" located at airports and major hotels, which you may charge on your Visa, Master, or Diner's card. You can also use your mobile telephone to place an overseas call.

You can use one of the following companies to access an international line. Rates vary, but Japan Telecom and IDC are generally lower than KDD:

KDD (Kokusai Denshin Denwa)	**001** (**002** for call-back on charges)
Japan Telecom	**0041** (0045)
IDC (Digital Communications)	**0061** (0062)

Direct dial the access number first, then the country code, area code, and telephone number.

For operator-assisted calls, station-to-station calls, person-to-person calls, and collect calls, dial **0051** (KDD).

If you need to find a phone number, call KDD Information Center (toll free) at **0057**, available 24 hours a day.

You can call toll free from green and gray public phones. Insert either ¥10 or a phone card before dialing. The coin or card will be returned when you hang up. To charge a credit card call through your regular long-distance carrier at home (a surcharge may apply), dial **0055**, or KDD's Home Country Direct at **0039**, Japan Telecom's Dial Abroad at **0043**, or IDC's Country Direct at **0066-55**, then add the following numbers:

AT&T's USA Direct	**111**
MCI's Call USA	**121**
Sprint's Sprint Express (USA)	**131**

Australia Direct (TELSTRA)	**611**
Call Home Australia (OPTUS)	**612**
Hong Kong Direct	**852**
UK Direct	**441** or **444**
Hawaii	**111** or **181**
Canada	**161**
Thailand	**661**
Singapore	**651**
South Korea	**821** or **822**
France	**331**
Italy	**391**

Because of the time difference, you can reach people at your home office in North America after midnight or between 6 AM and 8 AM Japan Time (see the time conversion chart on p. 173). Calls are charged in 6-second units. Economy rates run from 7 to 11 PM weekdays and 8 to 11 PM on weekends and holidays. Greater late-night discounts run daily from 11 PM to 8 AM.

EMERGENCIES

You can call the following numbers from any phone (operators are Japanese but will respond to calls in English if you speak slowly). You don't need a ¥10 coin to call these numbers at public phones, but you must push the red button on the phone before dialing.

Police	**110**
Fire/Ambulance	**119**

You will need a coin to call the following:

Police in English	**(03) 3501-0110** (Tokyo)
	8:30 AM to 5:15 PM (weekdays)
Hospital Information	
in Japanese	**(03) 3212-2323** (24 hours)

Hospital Information in English, Spanish, Chinese, Korean, Thai	**(03) 5285-8181** (24 hours)
The Japan Helpline	**(0120) 46-1997** (toll free)
TELL (Tokyo English Life Line)	**(03) 5774-0992**

Hotel personnel can connect you with English-speaking doctors and hospitals. Hospital reception desks are usually open from 8:30 to 11 AM weekdays. Some hospitals with English-speaking doctors are:

Tokyo

International Catholic Hospital (Seibo Byōin)	**(03) 3951-1111** (24 hours)
International Medical Center of Japan	**(03) 3202-7181**
	(03) 3207-1038 (Fax)
Japanese Red Cross (Hiroo Byōin) Medical Center	**(03) 3400-1311** (24 hours)
St. Luke's International Hospital (Seiroka Kokusai Byōin)	**(03) 3541-5151** (24 hours)
Tokyo Adventist Hospital (Tokyo Eisei Byōin)	**(03) 3392-6151** (9 AM to 5:30 PM)

Osaka

Osaka National Hospital	**(06) 942-1331** (8:30 AM to 6 PM)
	(06) 442-1334/5 (6 PM to 8:30 AM)
Sumitomo Hospital	**(06) 6443-1261**
	(8:30 to 11:30 AM, 12:30 to 3 PM)

OTHER USEFUL PHONE NUMBERS

Travel and Tourist Information in English
    (0088) 22-4800

Airport Flight Information
    New Tokyo International **(0476) 34-5000** (5:30 AM to 11 PM)
    Haneda **(03) 5757-8111** (5:30 AM to 11 PM)
    Osaka **(06) 6856-6781** (6:30 AM to 9:30 PM)
    Kansai International **(0724) 55-2500** (24 hours)

AIDS Hotline
    (0120) 46-1995

Tourist Information Centers

Tourist Information Centers (TICs), a service of the Japan National Tourist Organization, are conveniently located in airports and at downtown locations. Staff there can help foreign travelers, answer travel questions, suggest itineraries, offer maps and brochures on tourist destinations and cultural activities, and arrange for home visits. TICs do not make hotel reservations. If you have a free afternoon or day, they are an excellent place to gather information.

TOKYO
Kōtsū Kaikan Bldg., 10F
10-1, Yurakuchō 2-chōme
Chiyoda-ku, Tokyo 100-0006
Tel: (03) 3201-3331
9 AM to 5 PM weekdays
9 AM to 12 PM Saturdays

NARITA: PASSENGER TERMINAL 1
Tel: (0476) 30-3383
9 AM to 8 PM daily

NARITA: PASSENGER TERMINAL 2
Tel: (0476) 34-6251
9 AM to 8 PM daily

KANSAI INTERNATIONAL
Arrival Lobby, North Side, 1F
Sennan-gun, Osaka 549-0011
Tel: (0724) 56-6025
9 AM to 9 PM daily

KYOTO
Kyoto Tower Bldg., 1F
Shichijō-Karasuma Sagura
Shimogyō-ku, Kyoto 600-8216
Tel: (075) 371-5649
9 AM to 5 PM weekdays
9 AM to 12 PM Saturdays

Embassies (Tokyo)

AUSTRALIA
1-14, Mita 2-chōme
Minato-ku, Tokyo 108-8361
Tel: (03) 5232-4111
Fax: (03) 5232-4149

UNITED KINGDOM
1, Ichiban-chō
Chiyoda-ku, Tokyo 102-8381
Tel: (03) 5211-1100
Fax: (03) 5275-0346

CANADA
3-38, Akasaka 7-chōme
Minato-ku, Tokyo 107-8503
Tel: (03) 5412-6200
Fax: (03) 5412-6247

UNITED STATES
10-5, Akasaka 1-chōme
Minato-ku, Tokyo 107-8420
Tel: (03) 3224-5000
Fax: (03) 3224-5856

Consulates (Osaka)

AUSTRALIA
Twin 21 MID Tower, 29F
1-61, Shiromi 2-chōme
Chūō-ku, Osaka 540-6129
Tel: (06) 6941-9448
Fax: (06) 6920-4543

CANADA
Daisan Shoho Bldg., 12F
2-3, Nishi Shinsaibashi
2-chōme
Chūō-ku, Osaka 542-0086
Tel: (81) 6212-4910
Fax: (81) 6212-4914

UNITED KINGDOM
Seikō Osaka Bldg., 19F
5-1, Bakuro-machi 3-chōme
Chūō-ku, Osaka 541-0059
Tel: (06) 6282-1984
Fax: (06) 6282-1985

UNITED STATES
11-5, Nishi Tenma 2-chōme
Kita-ku, Osaka 530-8543
Tel: (06) 6315-5900
Fax: (06) 6315-5914

GOING ONLINE

Your laptop, modem, and basic e-mail account on the Internet will allow you to connect with your office back home. The hotel you are staying in should have all the jacks and connections you need, but if you have any difficulty finding access numbers or other information, contact one of the user groups listed below. ▲ *Be aware that access numbers and Internet addresses change frequently.*

SERVICE FOR YOUR LAPTOP

All major U.S. and European computer and computer peripheral companies have branch or representative offices in Japan, almost all of which are located in Tokyo. Ask the business center at your hotel, or call the office of the maker of your laptop for information on where to get it serviced.

HOTELS

Japan has a wide assortment of Japanese-style inns (**ryokan**) and Western-style hotels, from modest pensions and business hotels to deluxe international hotels. The best hotel choices for business travelers in Japan are:

- Category 1: First-class hotels in choice locations (roughly ¥36,000 to ¥60,000 per night for singles and doubles).

- Category 2: Deluxe business hotels in choice locations (roughly ¥22,000 to ¥32,000 for singles and doubles).

- Category 3: Ordinary business hotels, often in suburban areas (roughly ¥8,000 to ¥12,000 for singles and doubles). As a rule, ordinary business hotels serve more male guests, though women need not feel uncomfortable as most are quite clean and safe. Many of these hotels might not accept credit cards, so be prepared to pay cash on arrival.

The above prices do not include service charge or tax.

HOTELS WITH BUSINESS SERVICES

Most major hotels in Tokyo and Osaka have "business centers" where you can do photocopying, have material translated, use a computer, modem, or fax, have business cards made, hire an interpreter, arrange for courier service, rent meeting rooms, and so on. Usage is generally restricted to guests and prices vary. Be sure to check the list of available amenities before making or accepting reservations, particularly if you will be working out of your room.

TOKYO: BEST-KNOWN CENTRALLY LOCATED HOTELS

Imperial Hotel
1-1, Uchisaiwai-chō 1-chōme
Chiyoda-ku, Tokyo 100-8558
Tel: (03) 3504-1111
Fax: (03) 3581-9146

Hotel Okura
10-4, Toranomon 2-chōme
Minato-ku, Tokyo 105-0001
Tel: (03) 3582-0111
Fax: (03) 3582-3707

The New Otani
4-1, Kioi-chō
Chiyoda-ku, Tokyo 102-8578
Tel: (03) 3265-1111
Fax: (03) 3221-2619

Palace Hotel
1-1, Marunouchi 1-chōme
Chiyoda-ku, Tokyo 100-0005
Tel: (03) 3211-5211
Fax: (03) 3211-6987

TOKYO: HOTEL SAMPLING

Category 1: First-class Hotel

Park Hyatt (opened 1994)
7-1-2, Nishi Shinjuku 3-chōme
Shinjuku-ku, Tokyo 163-1055
Tel: (03) 5322-1234
Fax: (03) 5322-1288

- location: 15-minute walk from Shinjuku Station
- description: 52 stories, 178 rooms (39–52 Fl.); ultra-modern, high-tech on the outside; comfortable on the inside
- service: personalized, like a small hotel
- rooms: modern, Japanese-style decor with CD/laser disk player, fax machine, private voicemail
- bathroom: TV, heated toilet seat, built-in blow-dryer

Category 2: Deluxe Business Hotel

Tokyo Prince Hotel (built in 1964)
3-1, Shiba-kōen 3-chōme
Minato-ku, Tokyo 105-8560
Tel: (03) 3432-1111
Fax: (03) 3434-5551

- location: excellent; close to Shinbashi, Shinagawa, Roppongi, and Tokyo Tower

- description: 11 stories, 482 rooms; functional, with 28 banquet halls, 9 meeting rooms with a business center, and inexpensive restaurants
- service: good; you can get a reduction in your room rate if you stay for more than two days and accept less frequent changes of linen
- rooms: telephone, TV with movies and CNN
- bathroom: bathtub and amenities

Category 3: Ordinary Business Hotel

Tokyo Hotel Urashima
5-23, Harumi 2-chōme
Chūō-ku, Tokyo 104-0053
Tel: (03) 3533-3111
Fax: (03) 3533-5336

- location: 15 minutes from JR Tokyo Station or Tokyo City Air Terminal (TCAT or Hakozaki) by car
- description: 974 rooms plus 5 Japanese-style; modest but nice
- service: Japanese, continental, and Chinese restaurants; fax and word processor available
- rooms: very small but clean, TV, telephone, air conditioning
- bathroom: minimal

OSAKA: BEST-KNOWN HOTELS, LOCATED NEAR THE CENTRAL BUSINESS DISTRICTS

Osaka Hilton International
8-8, Umeda 1-chōme
Kita-ku, Osaka 530-0001
Tel: (06) 6347-7111
Fax: (06) 6347-7001

Plaza Osaka
9-15, Shin-Kitano 1-chōme
Yodogawa-ku, Osaka 532-0025
Tel: (06) 6303-1000
Fax: (06) 6303-0550

Rihga Royal Hotel
3-68, Nakanoshima 5-chōme
Kita-ku, Osaka 530-0005
Tel: (06) 6448-1121
Fax: (06) 6448-4414

Hotel New Otani Osaka
4-1, Shiromi 1-chōme
Chūō-ku, Osaka 540-8578
Tel: (06) 6941-1111
Fax: (06) 6941-9769

Hotel Nikkō Osaka
3-3, Nishi Shinsaibashi 1-chōme
Chūō-ku, Osaka 542-0086
Tel: (06) 6244-1111
Fax: (06) 6245-2432

Westin Osaka
1-20, Oyodo Naka 1-chōme
Kita-ku, Osaka 531-0076
Tel: (06) 6440-1111
Fax: (06) 6440-1100

OSAKA: HOTEL SAMPLING

Category 1: First-class Hotel

Nankai South Tower Hotel
1-60, Nanba 5-chōme
Chūō-ku, Osaka 542-0076
Tel: (06) 6646-1111
Fax: (06) 6632-5061

- location: excellent; connected to Nankai Nanba Station, in the entertainment area of Osaka—10 minutes from Umeda, the corporate hub, by subway and 29 minutes by express from Kansai International Airport

- description: 548 rooms, 11 international restaurants and cocktail lounges, 18 banquet rooms, and a business center

- service: deluxe, including baggage handling service from hotel to Nanba Station

- rooms: international telephone, cable TV, 24-hour room service

- bathroom: full amenities

Category 2: Deluxe Business Hotel

ANA Hotel Osaka (Osaka Zenniku Hotel)
3-1, Dojimahama 1-chōme
Kita-ku, Osaka 530-0004
Tel: (06) 6347-1112
Fax: (06) 6348-9208

- location: one hour from Kansai Airport by car, 10 minutes from JR Shin-Osaka station by car, a 10-minute walk from JR Osaka Station, and a 5-minute walk from Yodoyabashi Subway Station

- description: 23 stories, 498 rooms, 6 restaurants, 2 cocktail lounges, and 11 banquet rooms

- service: excellent, including fax line connected to each room

- rooms: deluxe

- bathroom: all amenities

Category 3: Ordinary Business Hotel

Rihga Royal Hotel Yotsūbashi
10-12, Shinmachi 1-chōme
Nishi-ku, Osaka 550-0013
Tel: (06) 6534-1211
Fax: (06) 6534-6360

- location: one hour by car from Kansai Airport, or use limousine to Hotel Nikkō Osaka, from which it's a 5-minute walk; 3-minute walk from Yotsubashi Subway Station

- description: 5 banquet rooms

Spend your evening at the Osaka Airport Hotel (576 rooms, 8 restaurants and bars) at the Kansai International Airport if you **OSAKA HOTEL TIP** *are connecting to other cities the following morning. It is a bit pricey, but you will save an hour of travel time, as the hotel is but a short walk from the air terminal. However, you should stay in town if you want to sample Osaka's substantial nightlife.*

- service: card-key system
- rooms: television, message telephone
- bathroom: minimal

MAKING HOTEL RESERVATIONS

Reservations should be made at least one month in advance of your trip, especially if you are visiting Tokyo or Kyoto where suitable accommodations can be scarce. JNTO can help you by providing information and advice.

DISCOUNT HOTEL COUPONS

Check with your travel agent about special room rates for some major hotels. Discount coupon plans available include:

- Japan Hotel Pass, good for 46 hotels in 24 cities, available through Nippon Travel agencies
- Kintetsu International Stay & Save Hotel Plan, good for 11 hotels in 4 cities, available through Kintetsu International Tours
- Special Hotel Rates for FITs, good for 200 hotels in 7 cities, available through Tōkyū Travel

Airlines may have special discount plans tied in with business-class flights.

WELCOME INNS

If you want to reserve an ordinary business hotel (category three) for under ¥8,000 per night, contact:

Welcome Inns Reservation Center
E gallery, Bldg. 1, 1F
Tokyo International Forum

Traditional Japanese Inns: *Ryokan*

Gaining Entry

Do not consider staying in a *ryokan* unless it has been recommended to you by someone who will help you with the arrangements. Without a Japanese paving the way with a guarantee that you are not a typical foreigner and will not disrupt the tranquillity of the inn, you will have little chance of gaining entry to a top-quality *ryokan*, which can cost easily as much as a first-class hotel. Each person is charged, based on double occupancy. Breakfast and dinner, often very elaborate, are included. The Japan National Tourist Organization's *Japan Ryokan Guide* lists more than 2,000 *ryokan*, all members of the Japan Ryokan Association.

Resistance to Foreign Guests

Ryokan may not welcome you because they fear they will not be able to understand your needs. Many believe that foreigners will not follow the customs and rules of the inn, thereby inconveniencing other guests.

5-1, Marunouchi 3-chōme
Chiyoda-ku, Tokyo 100-0006
Tel: (03) 3211-4201
Fax: (03) 3211-9009

The office is open from 9:15 AM to 12 PM and 1 PM to 5:15 PM weekdays. Lower-priced *ryokan* (Japanese-style inns) and *minshuku* (Japanese equivalent of bed-and-breakfast) are also available. JNTO offers a "Directory of Welcome Inns" that has a reservation request form on the back.

Baths

Public baths are called *sentō*, and hotel/home baths are called *ofuro*. Hot springs are called *onsen* (though the baths themselves are *ofuro*). One typical complaint is that foreigners soap up in the bath. When taking a Japanese bath, first wash outside of the bath, rinse well, and then get in; the *ofuro* is only for soaking and relaxing. The same bath water is used for all guests, so if someone contaminates the bath with soap, the water must be changed. If the tub is wooden, it has to be scrubbed before it is refilled.

Slippers

There are two kinds of slippers at *ryokan*, regular slippers for wooden floors and bathroom slippers for the bathroom floor. Another complaint is that foreigners forget to take off the bathroom slippers when they leave the bathroom area. This is considered unhygienic and may result in the owners washing the wooden floors. The bathroom slippers should be left in the bathroom for the next person to use.

ABOUT JAPANESE FOOD

Dinner with your Japanese associates is a *de rigueur* extension of the business day, and invitations should be accepted. Your hosts will go out of their way to take you somewhere with class, and, if it is their home cuisine, will delight in introducing you to some uniquely Japanese dishes. Turnabout is fair play, so you may also have occasion to invite them out. In addition to the regular categories of restaurants, there are special drinking places where you can savor a variety of small dishes along with beer, sake, or scotch and water (*mizu-*

wari, the preferred drink of many salarymen). These include Western-style beer halls and *nomiya*, Japanese-style drinking places with a red lantern (*akachōchin*) out front. Steer clear of "snack" bars, unless invited by your hosts, as they provide hostesses along with their drinks and can be very expensive.

For breakfast or lunch, you may occasionally find yourself on your own. Large hotel coffee shops and restaurants will make you feel right at home, but you may wish to venture out. You will not be entirely lost, however, as most lower- to upper-middle-end restaurants have plastic food displays in their windows.

JAPANESE CUISINE

Lauded as one of the world's healthiest cuisines, traditional Japanese cuisine is low in fat (though high in salt) and utilizes a wealth of different seafoods and fresh vegetables. A typical home-cooked meal consists of steamed rice, miso soup, Japanese pickles, and a main dish of fish or meat and vegetables. Formal meals, *kaiseki ryōri*, include a number of vegetable and fish dishes with seaweed- or mushroom-seasoned bases, each prepared in a different way—raw, boiled, broiled, deep fried, steamed, vinegared, or pickled/preserved. Presentation, which is exquisite, is enhanced by service in a variety of china and pottery dishes. Other restaurant fare, though perhaps not as nutritious as homemade, or decorative (and expensive) as *kaiseki*, nonetheless offers delicious variety.

Breakfast

Japanese are fast forgoing the traditional breakfast of grilled fish, miso soup, and rice for toast and cereal. For businesspeople on the go, one favorite is the *mōningu sābisu* ("morning service") breakfast served in coffee shops until 10 or 11 AM comprising rolls or thick, white-bread toast, a boiled egg, and a small salad with coffee or tea.

Lunch

Here is a selection of fast lunch favorites:

Bentō ("box lunches"), shallow boxes of cold, pressed rice with a variety of condiments on the side such as salmon, chicken, Japanese pickles, and **kamaboko** (pressed fish cakes). **Obentō** (with the honorific **o**), equivalent to the American bag lunch, are prepared at home or purchased at stores and fast-food **bentō** shops.

Teishoku ("set meals"), a fish or meat dish, pickles, rice, and miso soup often served together on a tray.

Onigiri, triangular, palm-sized rice balls with a pickled plum or other seasoned condiment in the middle, wrapped in a sheet of **nori** seaweed.

Sandwiches may contain ham or cheese but are just as likely to hold spaghetti, potato salad, or mandarin orange slices and whipped cream.

Donburi, a bowl of rice topped with chicken, chicken and egg, pork cutlet, or beef with onions.

Soba, buckwheat noodles in a fish-based broth with toppings such as fried tofu or tempura shrimp. (**Zaru-soba**, cold noodles with a light dipping sauce, is a traditional favorite—great during the hot, humid summers.)

Udon, thick white noodles in fish-based broth with a variety of toppings.

Rāmen, thin, Chinese-style noodles in a pork- or chicken-based broth with toppings of sliced pork, bean sprouts, spinach, and other condiments.

Yakisoba, soft, stir-fried ***rāmen*** noodles with chopped vegetables (usually carrots and cabbage) and a sprinkling of pork or seafood.

Yasai itame, stir-fried vegetables with bits of pork or seafood. If you do not want meat in your dish, say *"**niku nashi**"* ("without meat"), or *"**yasai dake**"* ("vegetables only").

Gyōza, the moon-shaped Japanese version of the Chinese pot sticker.

Donburi, soba, and ***udon*** are available at soba shops, which often have traditional Japanese interiors. Some shops feature stand-up counters only, where quick bowls of ***soba*** or ***udon*** can be consumed on the run. ***Rāmen, yakisoba, yasai itame,*** and ***gyōza*** are served at ***rāmen*** shops.

Dinner

Oden, a variety of pressed fish cakes, ***konbu*** seaweed, potatoes, ***konnyaku*** (devil's tongue paste), boiled eggs, and *fu* (wheat gluten cakes) stewed in a slightly sweet fish-based broth.

Sashimi, slices of raw fish.

Shabu-shabu, thinly sliced beef swished through boiling water with tofu and vegetables, then dipped in sauces. Noodles are cooked in the remaining broth.

Sukiyaki, sliced beef, tofu, vegetables, and thin bean-thread (***harusame***) noodles prepared in a frying pan (sometimes in front of restaurant guests) and traditionally served with a raw-egg dip.

Vending machines are everywhere and sell everything from soft drinks and rice to condoms, girlie magazines, **SELF-SERVICE FOOD (& MORE)**
bouquets, jewelry, and designer ties. You can also buy cold beer, warm sake, or whiskey from a vending machine until 11 PM. Convenience stores like 7-11 sell quick snacks, sandwiches, and sundries.

Sushi, rectangular, mouth-sized slices of raw fish on top of rice, with *wasabi* (Japanese horseradish) in between.

Tempura, deep-fried shrimp, yam, carrots, and other fish and vegetables. The nicer restaurants will add a deep-fried chrysanthemum leaf.

Tonkatsu, breaded pork cutlets served with shredded cabbage.

Unajū, rice topped with broiled eel (tastes much better than it sounds!).

Yakiniku. Korean-style meat you broil yourself over a grill at the table. Kimchi (Korean pickles) complement the meal.

Yakitori, chicken on bamboo skewers, grilled with salt (*shio-yaki*) or a teriyaki-type sauce (*tare-yaki*).

Good standbys: If you need an informal, cheap meal, go for the curry rice (*karē raisu)* or beef stew (*bīfu shichū*)—every restaurant makes them exactly the same way.

CHOICE RESTAURANTS

Here are several restaurants recommended for entertaining your Japanese associates (although normally you will be the guest). Restaurants may be closed between lunch and dinner. Always telephone first. Some older, traditional restaurants and small eateries may not accept traveler's checks or credit cards.

TOKYO

Tokyo is a bit like New York; you can find just about anything. Many Japanese enjoy fine European-style cuisine, and there are many restaurants that serve the more typically Japanese foods like sushi and tempura.

Bistro Trente-Trois (33). French. Inexpensive. The best French food for the money in town. Informal, but what it lacks in ambience it makes up for in the attention of its staff. Address: Bell Bldg., 1F, 27-1, Nishi Ikebukuro 3-chōme, Toshima-ku. Tel: **(03) 3986-7487**. Open 11:30 AM to 2 PM and 5:30 to 9:30 PM. Closed Sundays.

Brasserie Bernard. French. Moderate. Good, solid bourgeois French cooking in a homey atmosphere. Address: Kajimaya Bldg. 7F, 14-3, Roppongi 7-chōme, Minato-ku. Tel: **(03) 3405-7877**. Open 11:30 AM to 2 PM and 5:30 to 11:30 PM (evenings only on Sundays and holidays).

Otako Honten. Country-style Japan. Inexpensive. Has the feel of a Parisian bistro, but the house specialty is *oden*, a traditional Japanese "stew." Good place to unwind. Address: 4-16, Ginza 5-chōme, Chūō-ku. Tel: **(03) 3571-0057**. Open 4:30 to 11 PM. Closed Sundays and holidays.

Iseju. Classical Japanese. Moderate. A 125-year-old institution with an old-fashioned way of cooking and serving. House specialities are *sukiyaki* and *shabu-shabu*. Private tatami rooms are good for holding discussions. Address: 14-9, Nihonbashi Kodenmachō, Chūō-ku. Tel: **(03) 3663-7841**. Open 11 AM to 10:00 PM. Closed Sundays and holidays.

Maisen. *Tonkatsu* (pork cutlet). Inexpensive. The pork cutlet here is known as the best in Tokyo. A good place to go with associates you know well. Informal. Address: 8-5, Jingūmae 4-chōme, Shibuya-ku. Tel: **03-3470-0071**. Open 11 AM to 10 PM daily.

Kakiden. Japanese haute cuisine. Expensive, but worth it. Offers the formal, sophisticated cuisine called *kaiseki* without bankrupting you. *Koto* (Japanese harp) music provides a pleasant atmosphere.

Address: Yasuyo Bldg. 8F, 37-11, Shinjuku 3-chōme, Shinjuku-ku. Tel: **(03) 3352-5121**. Open 11 AM to 9 PM daily.

OSAKA

Osaka is known for its specialties such as Osaka-style sushi (fish and sweet, vinegared rice pressed together in a wooden mold and then cut into square pieces) and tempura. The city's business links with the West have also made it a center for French cooking. The Dōtonbori River district in the southern part of the city has many inexpensive restaurants and pubs.

Ron. Kobe steak. Expensive. Renowned for the excellence of its meat. A five-minute walk from Osaka Station. Address: 10-2, Sonezaki Shinchi 1-chōme, Kita-ku. Tel: **(06) 6344-6664.** Open 11:30 AM to 2 PM and 5 to 9 PM. Closed Sundays.

Kitamura. Traditional Japanese. Moderate. Founded in 1881. Famous for sukiyaki and its beautiful setting in an old Japanese-style house. Excellent choice for business entertaining. Address: 16-27, Higashi Shinsaibashi 1-chōme, Chūō-ku. Tel: **(06) 6245-4129**. Open 4 to 10 PM. Closed Sundays and holidays.

Kushitaru. Japanese-style kebabs. Moderate. Well-known for its *yakitori* (grilled chicken and vegetables on skewers). Informal. Address: 15-3, Nishi Shinsaibashi 1-chōme, Chūō-ku. Tel: **(06) 6281-0365**. Closed Sundays and holidays.

Colosseo. Italian cuisine. Moderate to expensive. Pleasant, not too fancy. Good for business dinners. Great bread! Address: Osaka Norin Kaikan Bldg., 2-6, Minami Senba 3-chōme, Chūō-ku. Tel: **(06) 6252-2024**. Open 12 to 2 PM and 6 to 9:30 PM. Closed Sundays and holidays.

ASSOCIATIONS

There are many associations in Japan for English-speaking residents. They are places to network, find out about business and job opportunities, and even close deals. While their memberships are generally made up of people who live and work in Japan, they also offer information and contact opportunities for visiting businesspeople. Many include Japanese members who have spent time abroad and speak some English. All associations listed below are headquartered in Tokyo. Be aware that telephone and fax numbers change often and are sometimes the home numbers of a contact person. Updated information and other contact information and descriptions are generally available on the Internet. Use search engines to find them.

CHAMBERS OF COMMERCE

American Chamber of Commerce in Japan (ACCJ). Promotes commerce between the U.S. and Japan. The most prominent association for Americans in Tokyo, its corporate and individual memberships include many U.S. companies and executives, as well as some Japanese. Tel: **(03) 3433-5381**.

Australian Chamber of Commerce. Tel: **(03) 5214-0710**.

Canadian Chamber of Commerce. Tel: **(03) 3556-9566**.

PROFESSIONAL ORGANIZATIONS

American Society of Mechanical Engineers (ASME). The Tokyo branch keeps its members informed of the latest engineering developments. Tel: North America **(800) 843-2763**, outside North America **(973) 882-1167**.

Far East Society of Architects and Engineers (FESAE), Tokyo. Talks, seminars, and field trips keep its members up on the latest developments in architecture and design. Tel: **(03) 3267-7086,** Fax: **(03) 3267-7668**.

Foreign Executive Women (FEW), Tokyo. A networking and support group for foreign women in Japan who work in many different fields. Activities include seminars, weekly breakfast meetings with guest speakers, and Sunday brunch get-togethers for new members. Tel: **(090) 7216-5171,** Fax: **(03) 3528-3772.**

Forum for Corporate Communications (FCC). Holds dinner meetings with guest speakers for its foreign and Japanese membership, who work mainly in advertising, public relations, and marketing. FCC also offers workshops, publishes a newsletter, and conducts a yearly English-language advertising contest. Tel/Fax: **(03) 3753-4779**.

International Business Study Association (IBSA). Holds monthly get-together meetings, with guest speakers, for its Japanese and foreign businessperson membership. Tel: **(03) 3402-3622**, Fax: **(03) 3402-3246**.

International Computer Association (ICA). A networking organization with both company and individual memberships. Monthly meetings feature dinner speakers who discuss leading-edge computer developments. Web site: **www.ica.gol.com/index.html**.

International Women in Communications (IWIC). Offers its membership the opportunity to mix with monthly speakers from the communications field. Meetings are bilingual in Japanese and English. Tel: **(03) 3443-1275**.

Kaisha Society. The society's foreign members, who work in Japanese companies, meet every third Wednesday to exchange information and ideas. There is also a job-finding service. Tel: **(03) 5562-0382.**

Roppongi Bar Association (RBA). Open to people who work in the field of law. Members gather monthly to party and parley. The *RBA Newsletter* has a classified section listing job opportunities. Fax: **(03) 3211-8871.**

Society of Writers, Editors, and Translators (SWET). Membership includes company employees and freelancers who work in all areas, from advertising and publishing to reporting and interpreting. Fax: **(042) 320-5278**.

Toastmasters International. Groups throughout Japan allow Japanese and foreigners the opportunity to improve their speaking skills. Within District 76: Club 1674, **(03) 3362-0438**; Club 4334, **(03) 3408-2009**; Club 5153, **(03) 3783-9911.**

TRADE CENTERS

World Trade Center of Japan
World Trade Center Bldg., 37F
4-1, Hamamatsuchō 2-chōme
Minato-ku, Tokyo 105-6104
Tel: (03) 3435-5669
Fax: (03) 3436-4368

World Trade Center Osaka
WTC Bldg., 50F
14-16, Nankōkita 1-chōme
Suminoe-ku, Osaka 559-0034
Tel: (06) 6615-7000
Fax: (06) 6616-4130

Kobe Industrial Promotion Foundation
Kobe Industrial Promotion Center, 6F
8-4, Higashi Kawasaki-chō 1-chōme
Chūō-ku, Kobe 650-0044
Tel: (078) 360-3208
Fax: (078) 360-1419

TRADE ASSOCIATIONS

Japan Foreign Trade Council
World Trade Center Bldg.
4-1, Hamamatsuchō 2-chōme
Minato-ku, Tokyo 105-6106
Tel: (03) 3435-5952
Fax: (03) 3435-5969

Federation of Economic
Organizations (Keidanren)
Keidanren Kaikan
9-4, Ōtemachi 1-chōme
Chiyoda-ku, Tokyo 100-8188
Tel: (03) 5204-1500
Fax: (03) 5255-6255

Japan Federation of Importers
Organizations
Hogaku Bldg.
19-14, Toranomon 1-chōme
Minato-ku, Tokyo 105-0001
Tel: (03) 3581-9251
Fax: (03) 3581-9217

Japan External Trade
Organization (JETRO)
2-5, Toranomon 2-chōme
Minato-ku, Tokyo 105-8466
Tel: (03) 3582-5511
Fax: (03) 3587-0219

JETRO Foreign Access Zone
(FAZ)
Akasaka Twin Tower, 3F
17-22, Akasaka 2-chōme
Minato-ku, Tokyo 107-0052
Tel: (03) 3584-6021
Fax: (03) 3584-6024

CONVENTION FACILITIES

Venues abound for events and conventions, but reservations are hard to get and must be made far in advance. Each major city in Japan offers a variety of convention sites from which to choose. The Japan National Tourist Organization and affiliated Japan Convention Bureau offices provide information on venues and conventions due to be held. Individual city offices also provide some English-language information on their facilities.

TOKYO METROPOLITAN AREA

Chiba

Located in the northeast corner of Tokyo Bay, Chiba Prefecture, aggressively developed in recent years, contains one of Japan's largest and most popular convention centers, the Nippon Convention Center. Its International Exhibition Hall provides more than 54,000 m^2 of space. The Makuhari Messe Event Hall accommodates 9,000, the Convention Hall 2,000, and the International Conference Room 688. Mid-sized and small meeting rooms accommodate 160–300 and 20–70 people, respectively. Contact:

Chiba Convention Bureau
Marine East, WBG, 14F
2-6 Nakase
Mihama-ku, Chiba 261-7114
Tel: (043) 297-5751
Fax: (043) 297-2753

Tokyo

Crowded as it is, Tokyo has a great multipurpose exhibition space practically at its center—Tokyo Dome. During the baseball off-season (the Yomiuri Giants play here), the Dome sports everything from concerts to orchid festivals in its 46,755 m^2 space, with event seating for 62,000. Contact the Information Center at **(03) 5800-9999** or:

Japan Convention Bureau/Japan National Tourist Organization
10-1, Yūrakuchō 2-chōme
Chiyoda-ku, Tokyo 100-0006
Tel: (03) 3216-2905
Fax: (03) 3216-7680

Yokohama

This busy port city and popular convention site, less than an hour from Tokyo by train, has many new developments along Tokyo Bay, including Minato Mirai (MM21), the "Future Port of the 21st Century." The Pacifico Yokohama (Pacific Convention Plaza Yokohama), the largest convention complex of its kind in Japan, includes a conference center that accommodates up to 1,500 and a 10,000 m^2 exhibition hall. Its auditorium seats 5,000. Contact:

Convention Division
Pacifico Yokohama, 5F
1-1, Minato Mirai
Nishi-ku, Yokohama 220-0012
Tel: (045) 221-2111
Fax: (045) 221-2100

FUKUOKA

Kyushu's principal center of commerce, Fukuoka, known for its ambience and easy access from other parts of Japan, is building more international convention centers. Present facilities include mammoth, multipurpose Fukuoka Dome with a capacity of 52,000, Fukuoka International Center with a capacity of 10,000, and a new Exhibition Hall with a capacity of 15,000. Contact:

Fukuoka Convention and Visitors Bureau
Fukuoka City Hall
North Annex, 5F
1-10-1 Tenjin
Chūō-ku, Fukuoka 810-0001
Tel: (092) 733-5050
Fax: (092) 733-5055

NAGOYA

Situated between Tokyo and Osaka, Nagoya is at the center of Japan's third-largest metropolitan area. It is noted for its high-tech auto, aerospace, and industrial robot industries. Convention facilities, plentiful and expanding, include the Nagoya International Exhibition Hall, with 33,946 m^2 of exhibition space, and the Nagoya Congress Center, with conference facilities for 3,012, and 3,270 m^2 of exhibition space. Contact:

Nagoya Convention and Visitors Bureau
Nagoya Chamber of Commerce and Industry Bldg., 5F
10-19, Sakae 2-chōme
Naka-ku, Nagoya 460-0008
Tel: (052) 202-1140
Fax: (052) 231-0922

NAGANO

Site of the 1998 Winter Olympics, Nagano is booming with new construction. Current facilities include the Nagano Skating Center with 10,318 m^2 of exhibition space and the Nagano Prefectural Culture Hall with conference capacities of 2,173, 1,070, and 285, respectively, in three halls. Contact:

Nagano Convention Bureau
22-2, Wakasato 3-chōme
Nagano-ku, Nagano 380-0928
Tel: (026) 223-6050
Fax: (026) 223-5520

NIIGATA

Situated on the Japan Sea coast, Niigata, a medium-sized city with an international airport, handles large-scale conventions in venues that include the Niigata Convention Center, with a hall holding 8,370, and a 1,320 m² exhibition space. Contact:

Niigata Visitors and Convention Bureau
Niigata City Public Development Corporation Bldg., 3F
1-613-69 Hakusan-ura
Niigata-shi, Niigata 951-8131
Tel: (025) 265-8000
Fax: (025) 266-3357

OSAKA

Formed by merchants, Osaka was Japan's first independent city. The New Kansai International Airport makes international travel to Osaka, which has a number of convention sites, even more convenient. Intex Osaka, recently upgraded, has 70,000 m² of exhibition space available in two halls. Osaka-jō Hall offers conference space for 5,000, and 3,500 m² of multipurpose space, while Mydome Osaka Hall offers 4,848 m² of exhibition space. Contact:

Osaka Convention Bureau
3-51, Nakanoshima 5-chōme
Kita-ku, Osaka 530-0005
Tel: (06) 6459-1771
Fax: (06) 6459-1773

SAPPORO

Capital of the northern island of Hokkaido, Sapporo has many convention sites. This "pioneer" city, settled from 1869, is best known for its yearly snow festival. Makomanai Ice Arena, the largest facility, has a conference hall with a capacity of 10,018, a 3,000 m² exhibition space, and several small meeting rooms. Contact:

Sapporo Convention Bureau
Sapporo International Communication Plaza
Sapporo MN Bldg., 3F
Kita 1 Nishi 3
Chūō-ku, Sapporo 060-001
Tel: (011) 211-3675
Fax: (011) 232-3833

TOILETS

Hotel and business office toilets are almost always Western-style, but you will occasionally come across squat toilets, particularly in train stations. Place your feet on either side of the ceramic bowl facing the "lip" portion. If you are wearing pants, watch your belt. If wearing a skirt, watch out for your hemline. Public rest rooms do not provide toilet paper or paper towels, so keep pocket tissues with you and a handkerchief to dry your hands. In women's rest rooms, which are often crowded, lines generally form in front of each stall.

You need to know three things about Japanese toilets: (1) what the small box with the push knob is, (2) that you are supposed to squat, not sit, and (3) when to carry your own toilet paper and handkerchief.

THE BOX

The small box along the wall of the toilet is there for you to use to cover up noise. Push the button on the box and it will make a noise similar to a flushing sound. It is customary for Japanese to flush the toilet several times in order to mask bathroom noises, and to conserve water, the noise box was invented.

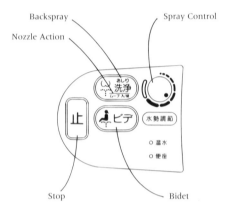

Instruction sheet posted on or near a Japanese "electric" toilet. Most hotels and facilities that cater to non-Japanese will have information posted in English, but in case they don't there is no reason you should be deprived of the pleasures and benefits of this amazing fixture. Just use this translation as a guide (be sure you commit the character for "stop" to memory before you begin).

Backspray

Spray Control

Nozzle Action

Stop

Bidet

SQUATTING

Squat over the toilet with a foot on each side. Usually there will be a bar or something you can hold onto in front of you—if you are on the high-speed bullet train, this is a must.

PAPER

You must carry tissue paper at all times because Japanese bathrooms frequently do not have any toilet paper. In addition, you must also carry a handkerchief because Japanese bathrooms frequently do not have paper towels. The big hotels, companies, and first-class restaurants will have paper products provided, but even in Tokyo, if you go to a second- or third-class restaurant, you could be in deep trouble if you are caught unprepared.

SPECIAL NOTE FOR WOMEN

If you are in a big city, you will most always find a Western-style toilet. However, if you are visiting factories or companies in rural Japan, you will have to learn the squatting technique and avoid, at all cost, pantyhose. One woman engineering director who frequently goes to Japan complained about how difficult the Japanese-style bathroom was and on her third trip to Japan found that the Japanese had installed a Western-style toilet just for her. More and more hotels and business buildings have plug-in toilet seats that warm you in winter. They may also have new, high-tech toilet seats with various buttons to push to cleanse and dry yourself. Instructions are in Japanese, which could lead to unwanted splashes, so a typical diagram with translations of key words is provided here.

Survival Japanese

WHY MAKE THE EFFORT?

It is important that you take the time to learn the correct pronunciation of Japanese. This will make a good impression and will also help avoid confusion. The good news here is that, although Japanese is a difficult language for most Westerners to learn, the pronunciation is easily mastered. This section will give you the basics. Practice and learn the correct pronunciation of proper names, especially the names of your Japanese associates. In casual conversation, try to use a few Japanese words and phrases, and then continue on in English. Your efforts will go a long way toward showing the sincerity of your desire to establish a good working relationship with the Japanese. Accept Japanese praise for your efforts with modesty, and always be sure that during important negotiations you have a trusted interpreter to assist you. The Japanese writing system is very complex, although here again your efforts to recognize familiar words will be much appreciated (and may help you when you're traveling around on your own).

PRONUNCIATION

JAPANESE VOWELS

There are five vowels in Japanese and each has only one pronunciation.

a	"ah"	as in "father" (not the **a** in "cat" or "ate")
i	"ee"	as in "machine" (not the **i** in "night" or "big")
u	"oo"	as in "true" (not the **u** in "mud" or "cute")
e	"eh"	as in "egg" (not the **e** in "me" or "free")
o	"oh"	as in "open" or "hope" (not the **o** in "not")

LONG/SHORT VOWELS

Long and short vowels are important because the meaning of a word can change according to the length of the vowel. Long vowels have the same pronunciation but are sounded twice as long as short vowels. They are indicated by a line over the vowel.

obasan	"aunt"	*obāsan*	"grandmother"
kibo	"scale"	*kibō*	"hope"
biru	"building"	*bīru*	"beer"

THE VOWELS I AND U

Vowels **i** and **u** are not pronounced when they appear between unvoiced consonants (f, h, k, p, s, t, ch, sh) or when **u** appears at the end of a sentence after an unvoiced consonant.

tabemasu	pronounced TA BE MAS	"eat"
ashita	pronounced A SH TA	"tomorrow"

JAPANESE CONSONANTS

Japanese consonants are pronounced exactly like English consonants with these exceptions:

f made by blowing air out between both lips rather than between the lower lip and teeth

Fujisan	"Mt. Fuji"	*ofuro*	"bath"

g as in "go" (not the g in "gentle")

tamago	"egg"	*gaijin*	"foreigner"

n a single **n** is a full syllable

pachinko	PA CHI N KO	"pinball"

r bears little resemblance to the English **r.** It is made by tapping the tongue once against the ridge right behind the front teeth, as in the English **d**.

rainen	"next year"	*rāmen*	"noodles"

DOUBLE CONSONANTS

When you see a double consonant, hold the first consonant before you continue sounding the word.

Roppongi	ROP [hold] PON GI
Nikkō	NIK [hold] KŌ
konnichi wa	KO N [hold] NI CHI WA
	"good afternoon"

USEFUL EXPRESSIONS

Hai.	Yes.
Iie.	No.
Ohayō gozaimasu.	Good morning. [morning greeting]
Konnichi wa.	Good afternoon. [daytime greeting]
Konban wa.	Good evening. [evening greeting]
Mata ashita.	See you tomorrow.
Sayōnara.	Good-bye.
Wakarimasu.	I understand.
Wakarimasen.	I don't understand.
Wakarimasu ka?	Do you understand?
Itadakimasu.	I receive. [said just before eating]
Gochisōsama deshita.	Thank you for the meal. [used by a guest after a meal]
Sumimasen.	Please excuse me.
Ojama shimasu.	Excuse me. [used on entering]
Shitsurei shimasu.	Excuse me. [used when leaving early or excusing oneself]
Omedetō gozaimasu.	Congratulations.
Yokatta desu.	Good.
Chigaimasu.	This/that is incorrect.
Machigaimashita.	I made a mistake.
Osoku narimashita.	I am late. Excuse me.
Ohisashiburi desu.	It's been a long time since I saw you last. (It's good to see you.)
Isogashii desu ka?	Are you busy? (Can I interrupt you?)

The Japanese writing system consists of two kana *syllabaries (representing sounds, not letters), with 46 characters each, and several* **WRITTEN JAPANESE** *thousand* kanji, *or Chinese characters. You will see the English alphabet used frequently in signs and advertising. Japanese can be written horizontally from left to right or vertically from top to bottom and right to left. Some common* kanji *characters of importance to travelers appear on p. 61.*

Isogashii desu ne!	You are so busy (therefore, doing well)!
Kentō shimashō.	Let's investigate (it).
Kangaete okimashō.	Let's put it aside and think about it.
Osewa ni narimashita.	I'm in your debt.
Otsukaresama.	You worked hard. [acknowledgment to someone at the end of the day or after a hard task]
Gokurōsama.	Thank you for going the extra mile. [said to someone below or equal to you in status who did something outstanding for you]
Dōzo.	Please (go ahead, take one, etc.)
Dōmo.	Thanks.
Arigatō.	Thank you.
Arigatō gozaimasu.	Thank you very much.

TIME WORDS

HOURS

ichi-ji	1 o'clock	*shichi-ji*	7 o'clock
ni-ji	2 o'clock	*hachi-ji*	8 o'clock
san-ji	3 o'clock	*ku-ji*	9 o'clock
yo-ji	4 o'clock	*jū-ji*	10 o'clock
go-ji	5 o'clock	*jūichi-ji*	11 o'clock
roku-ji	6 o'clock	*jūni-ji*	12 o'clock

The suffix *-kan* is added to indicate duration:

ichi-ji-kan	1 hour (long)	*go-ji-kan*	5 hours (long)

Useful Expressions *Kuizu*

What is the appropriate expression in each situation?

1. Upon opening the door to another person's office or home:
   (a) *Ojama shimasu.* (b) *Otsukaresama.*
   (c) *Omedetō gozaimasu.*

2. When you go over to someone's desk to discuss a project or to ask advice:
   (a) *Mata ashita.* (b) *Isogashii desu ka?* (c) *Konnichi wa.*

3. You are thanking a colleague for work he just did with you:
   (a) *Otsukaresama.* (b) *Ohisashiburi desu.*
   (c) *Ojama shimasu.*

4. You have arrived late to a meeting or appointment:
   (a) *Sumimasen.* (b) *Konnichi wa.* (c) *Ojama shimasu.*

5. A friend has been promoted, become engaged, or had a baby:
   (a) *Kentō shimashō.* (b) *Omedetō gozaimasu.*
   (c) *Gokurōsama.*

LAST, THIS, NEXT—DAY, WEEK, MONTH, YEAR

	LAST	THIS (PRESENT)	NEXT
day	*kinō*	*kyō*	*ashita*
week	*senshū*	*konshū*	*raishū*
month	*sengetsu*	*kongetsu*	*raigetsu*
year	*kyonen*	*kotoshi*	*rainen*

MINUTES

ip-pun	1 minute	*san-pun*	3 minutes

6. When leaving a meeting before others, a good departing greeting is:
   (a) *Shitsurei shimasu.* (b) *Dōmo.* (c) *Arigatō.*

7. When submitting a report that is late:
   (a) *Dōmo.* (b) *Kangaete okimashō.*
   (c) *Sumimasen. Osoku narimashita.*

8. A delivery man has just brought to your desk a package from another company. You should say:
   (a) *Arigatō gozaimasu.* (b) *Gokurōsama.*
   (c) *Kentō shimashō.*

9. Upon arriving at the office in the morning:
   (a) *Ohayō gozaimasu.* (b) *Konnichi wa.* (c) *Konban wa.*

10. Upon leaving the office for the day:
    (a) *Mata ashita.* b) *Arigatō.* (c) *Ojama shimasu.*

ANSWERS
1-a. 2-b. 3-a. 4-a. 5-b. 6-a. 7-c. 8-b. 9-a. 10-a.

ni-fun	2 minutes	*yon-fun*	4 minutes
go-fun	5 minutes	*hap-pun*	8 minutes
rop-pun	6 minutes	*kyū-fun*	9 minutes
nana-fun	7 minutes	*jup-pun*	10 minutes

DAYS

getsu-yōbi	Monday	*kin-yōbi*	Friday
ka-yōbi	Tuesday	*do-yōbi*	Saturday
sui-yōbi	Wednesday	*nichi-yōbi*	Sunday
moku-yōbi	Thursday		

MONTHS

ichi-gatsu	January	*shi-gatsu*	April
ni-gatsu	February	*go-gatsu*	May
san-gatsu	March	*roku-gatsu*	June
shichi-gatsu	July	*jū-gatsu*	October
hachi-gatsu	August	*jūichi-gatsu*	November
ku-gatsu	September	*jūni-gatsu*	December

UP-TO-DATE BUSINESS LOANWORDS

Japanese use many words borrowed from English that are already familiar to you. The problem is that these words no longer sound like English. They sound like Japanese. Learning how to pronounce and understand these "borrowed" words will immediately give you a more extensive Japanese vocabulary. To fine-tune your ear, keep in mind the following:

- because the basic syllable in Japanese consists of a consonant sound + a vowel, a Japanese speaker may add vowels to an English word: "cost" becomes *kosuto* (three syllables)

- the English **l** will translate into the Japanese **r** sound: "plus" becomes *purasu*

- the foreign word often gets shortened: "personal computer" becomes *paso-kon*

Here are some common loanwords used in Japanese business.

bijinesuman	businessman
dorafuto	draft
dorai	"dry," someone who is all business and not personable

furasutorēshon	frustration
furekishiburu	flexible
hōmupēji	homepage
intabyū	interview
intānetto	Internet
kone	connection/s
kosuto	cost
kyaria-ūman	career woman
mākechingu	marketing
masu-komi	"mass communications," media
ō-eru	O.L., "office lady," a woman who works in the office; used for non-career women who fill administrative positions
pēji	page
purinto	copy, handout
puroguramu	program
repōto	report
reshīto	receipt
risutora	restructuring
sararī-man	"salary man," white-collar worker
sekuhara	sexual harassment
sofuto	1. soft, 2. software content
takushī	taxi
uetto	"wet," someone who is friendly and wants to establish a good working relationship

Client Data

Client/company name _____

Address _____

_____

_____

City _____ Postal Code _____

Phone _____ Fax _____

E-mail _____ Web _____

Chief contacts

_____ title _____ ext_____

_____ title _____ ext_____

_____ title _____ ext_____

Section of town _____ Train line _____

Nearest station _____ Exit to use _____

Walking/Taxi directions _____

_____

_____

Notes _____

_____

_____

_____

_____

_____

_____

_____

_____

_____

_____

_____

Client Data

Client/company name _____

Address _____

_____

_____

City _____ Postal Code _____

Phone _____ Fax _____

E-mail _____ Web _____

Chief contacts

_____ title _____ ext_____

_____ title _____ ext_____

_____ title _____ ext_____

Section of town _____ Train line _____

Nearest station _____ Exit to use _____

Walking/Taxi directions _____

_____

_____

Notes _____

_____

_____

_____

_____

_____

_____

_____

_____

_____

_____

Gift Record

Gifts given

_____ to _____
_____ to _____
_____ to _____
_____ to _____
_____ to _____
_____ to _____
_____ to _____
_____ to _____
_____ to _____
_____ to _____
_____ to _____
_____ to _____
_____ to _____
_____ to _____

Gifts received

_____ from _____
_____ from _____
_____ from _____
_____ from _____
_____ from _____
_____ from _____
_____ from _____

North American Standard Time and DST vs. Japan Time

STANDARD TIME

→ ONE DAY BEHIND JAPAN   SAME DAY IN JAPAN →

EST	11	12	1	2	3	4	5	6	7	8	9	10
CST	10	11	12	1	2	3	4	5	6	7	8	9
MST	9	10	11	12	1	2	3	4	5	6	7	8
PST	8	9	10	11	12	1	2	3	4	5	6	7
JAPAN	1	2	3	4	5	6	7	8	9	10	11	12

DAYLIGHT SAVING TIME

→ ONE DAY BEHIND JAPAN   SAME DAY IN JAPAN →

EDST	12	1	2	3	4	5	6	7	8	9	10	11
CDST	11	12	1	2	3	4	5	6	7	8	9	10
MDST	10	11	12	1	2	3	4	5	6	7	8	9
PDST	9	10	11	12	1	2	3	4	5	6	7	8

bold italic type indicates PM

shaded area represents normal business hours in each time zone

Topic Finder

THE BRANNEN GROUP

Author CHRISTALYN BRANNEN spent the first 20 years of her life primarily in Japan. She attended Sophia University in Tokyo, earning her BA from the University of Texas at Austin and her MA at the University of California at Berkeley. She founded the Brannen Group in 1984 to provide consulting and cross-cultural training that would help businesses master the challenges of a multinational, multicultural marketplace. Today the Brannen Group's bilingual and bicultural staff has delivered more than 7,000 workshops and seminars to over 100 multinational corporations in more than a dozen countries. The company also offers leadership and management programs that address the challenges of communications, management business practices, influencing skills, teamwork, negotiations, and vendor relations.